John Henry Wright

**The date of Cylon**

A study in early Athenian history

John Henry Wright

**The date of Cylon**
*A study in early Athenian history*

ISBN/EAN: 9783337118600

Printed in Europe, USA, Canada, Australia, Japan

Cover: Foto ©ninafisch / pixelio.de

More available books at **www.hansebooks.com**

# THE DATE OF CYLON

## *A STUDY IN EARLY ATHENIAN HISTORY*

BY

JOHN HENRY WRIGHT

REPRINTED FROM THE HARVARD STUDIES IN CLASSICAL PHILOLOGY

VOL. III, 1892

BOSTON, U.S.A.

GINN AND COMPANY

1892

# THE DATE OF CYLON.

BY JOHN HENRY WRIGHT.

"Si in tantis temporum difficultatibus definire quidquam licet." — BOECKH.

## I.

## INTRODUCTORY.

THE fifty years preceding the legislation of Solon witnessed most significant changes in the political, social, and economic conditions of Athens, and in the relations of that little state to the world without. The main features of these changes were, as regards internal development, first, the dawning of popular political consciousness — the birth, from the throes of economic distress, of Democracy, — and, secondly, an increased intensity of factional feeling among the several families of the ruling Aristocracy ; and, as regards both domestic and foreign relations, we have to note the development of local industries and of foreign trade, *i.e.* the beginnings of the commercial enterprise which subsequently aided in giving Athens her political supremacy among the Greek states.

The dates of a few events in these and in earlier important movements have been preserved to us. If we are to place any confi-

NOTE. — This paper was originally prepared in 1888 and was read before the American Philological Association at the meeting of that year (*Proc. Am. Philol. Assoc.*, 1888, p. xxvi.) ; in the summer of 1890 it was rewritten for publication in the HARVARD STUDIES. Since that time, however, the important and long-lost treatise of Aristotle on the Athenian Commonwealth, recently discovered, has been published to the world, with its complete confirmation of the correctness of the writer's chief contention — a pre-Draconian date for Cylon. Instead of the fragments of this work, preserved in the Berlin Papyrus, No. CLXIII., and in a garbled form in the later Greek writers, we have now a copy of the original text, prepared probably not far from A.D. 100 (British Museum Papyrus, No. CXXXI.), to which to appeal. The paper has accordingly been revised, and in part rewritten, in the new light thus unexpectedly shed, not only upon the affair of Cylon, but also upon the whole subject of Athenian constitutional history before the time of Peisistratus. See F. D. Allen, *The Nation*, March 5, 1891 (No. 1340, pp. 197, 198).

dence in the recorded lists of Olympic and Pythian victors, of Attic archons, etc., — many of which were made up contemporaneously, — and in the chronological studies of ancient Greek scholars, which were based upon these lists, we must regard most of these dates as fairly well established.

Attic history opens with the rule of kings by right of birth; this early merges into that of kings by election, for such must we regard the so-called life-archons.[1] About the middle of the eighth century B.C.,[2] the last life-archon gives place to the decennial archon :[3] this is evidently a movement on the part of the aristocratic families in the direction of greater control. In the first half of the seventh century B.C.,[4] the decennial archontate is replaced by a board of nine

---

[1] The term βασιλεύς was applied to the life-archons and to the decennial archons down to the last Medontid, Hippomenes : Photius *Lex.*, (and Suidas) *s.v.* παρ' ἵππον καὶ κόρην · ... Ἱππομένης ... τελευταῖος ἐβασίλευεν. In Marmor Parium (Epp. 27, 28, 29, 30, 31) certain life-archons are named as kings: cf. Eusebius *Chron.* I. 188 *p* (Schöne), βασιλεύει Ἀλκμαίων. In fact, the name βασιλεύς was always retained (βασιλεύς alone is correct, not ἄρχων βασιλεύς: Hauvette-Besnault, *de Archonte Rege*, Paris, 1884, p. 1). Cf. Busolt, *Griech. Gesch.* I. 400, 401, and below, p. 30, note 2, for a discussion of the name by which the annual archons were probably designated before Solon's time. Once for all I wish here to express my debt to Busolt, not alone for his abundant bibliographical references, but also for the suggestion of many new points of view.

[2] The dates given for these events are those computed by the ancient chronographers, and may be regarded as fairly authentic, at least after contemporary records of Olympic victors, etc., were begun. These ἀναγραφαί seem to date as far back as the first half of the eighth century B.C. Euseb. *Chron.* I. 194: ἱστοροῦσι δὲ οἱ περὶ Ἀριστόδημον τὸν Ἠλεῖον ὡς ἀπ' εἰκοστῆς καὶ ἑβδόμης Ὀλυμπιάδος ... ἤρξαντο οἱ ἀθληταὶ ἀναγράφεσθαι ... πρὸ τοῦ γὰρ οὐδεὶς ἀνεγράφη ... τῇ δὲ εἰκοστῇ ὀγδόῃ τὸ στάδιον νικῶν Κόροιβος Ἠλεῖος ἀνεγράφη πρῶτος. καὶ ἡ Ὀλυμπιὰς αὕτη πρώτη ἐτάχθη, ἀφ' ἧς Ἕλληνες ἀριθμοῦσι τοὺς χρόνους. τὰ δ' αὐτὰ τῷ Ἀριστοδήμῳ καὶ Πολύβιος ἱστορεῖ. *Ibid.* 192, ἀπὸ γὰρ τούτων τὰ τῆς Ἑλλήνων χρονογραφίας ἀκριβοῦς ἀναγραφῆς τετευχέναι δοκεῖ · τὸ πρὸ αὐτῶν, ὡς ἑκάστῳ φίλον ἦν, ἀνεφήναντο. On the ἀναγραφαί (Macedonian, Argive, Sicyonian, Halicarnassian, etc.), see Busolt, *G. G.* I. 137, note 2. Mahaffy's arguments for a later date (about 580 B.C.) for the Olympian register do not convince me (*Journ. Hellen. Stud.* 2 [1881], pp. 164–178).

[3] B.C. 752/1, according to Dionysius of Halicarnassus (*Ant.* I. 71 and 75), Julius Africanus and Eusebius (I. 187 *p*, *q*), probably based upon Eratosthenes-Apollodorus.

[4] B.C. 682/1 (Ol. 24. 3), according to Dionysius Halic., Julius Africanus, and Eusebius, here likewise apparently following the system of Eratosthenes as elabo-

chief magistrates annually chosen. According to the recently discovered treatise on the Athenian Commonwealth, this board was
historically developed in the following way :[1] at a very early date the
office of Polemarch ('Field-marshal'), and afterwards that of Archon
('Regent'), were established for the purpose of providing coadjutors
for the King; very much later — when the elections became annual
— this board of three was enlarged by the addition of the six Thesmothetae. At some date not to be determined, perhaps not before
the time of Solon, but possibly when the archontate became annual,
the Archon took precedence of the King and this precedence was
ever afterward retained. All these changes in the nature and tenure
of the chief magistracy clearly testify to the increasing influence of
the leading families, seeking to limit and circumscribe, as far as might
be, the power of rivals in office. It should be remembered that
throughout these times, and probably for long afterward, the privilege
of election to this board of officials belonged for the most part to
the nobles, commonly called Eupatrids, and that the number of families constituting this class was not large. In the seventh century B.C.
Athens was a community of ancient and powerful families, with social
and political conditions very different from those that prevailed subsequently.

The archontate, at least before the time of Solon, and to a certain
extent in the sixth century B.C., though then somewhat shorn of its
powers, was not only nominally but actually the highest office in
the state ; it combined the widest executive and judicial functions,
and was the prize eagerly sought after by the ambitious.[2] The

---

rated by Apollodorus. Mar. Par. (Ep. 32) gives B.C. 683/1. Syncellus, p. 399,
21, *i.e.* Jul. Africanus: μετὰ τούτους ἄρχοντες ἐνιαυσιαῖοι ἡρέθησαν ἐξ εὐπατριδῶν,
ἐννέα τε ἀρχόντων 'Αθήνησιν ἀρχὴ κατεστάθη (cf. Euseb. *Chron.* II. 84, 85).
The chronographer whom Pausanias follows (IV. 5. 10 and 13. 7) puts the beginning of the annual archontate in B.C. 687/6. For an explanation of this fluc-
tuation in dates, see Gelzer, *Hist. u. Philol. Aufsätze E. Curtius gewidmet*, 1884,
p. 20; his best example, however, has lost its value, now that Damasias is known
to belong to the sixth, not the seventh, century B.C. For further literature, see
Busolt, *G. G.* I. 407.

[1] Aristotle, *Respublica Atheniensium*, c. 3 (Kenyon).

[2] Thuc. I. 126: τότε δὲ τὰ πολλὰ τῶν πολιτικῶν οἱ ἐννέα ἄρχοντες ἔπρασσον·
Aristot. *Respub. Ath.* c. 13: δῆλον ὅτι μεγίστην εἶχεν δύναμιν ὁ ἄρχων· φαίνονται
γὰρ ἀεὶ στασιάζοντες περὶ ταύτης τῆς ἀρχῆς. Also probably Herod. V. 71 : οἱ πρυ-

archons in this period are commonly men of note and importance,[1] —
not the figureheads of the fifth and later centuries, when the choice
was by lot from a considerable number of selected persons,[2] — and
their election attested the triumphs of family or of political factions,
thus having something of the significance that attached to the election of generals in the age of Pericles and in the Peloponnesian war.[3]

The most important datable event following the establishment of
the annual archontate — leaving out of the question for the present
that which is the subject of our enquiry — is the legislation of Draco,
in Ol. 39, probably B.C. 621.[4]  At this time, besides the enactment of

---

τάνιες τῶν ναυκράρων οἵπερ ἔνεμον τότε τὰς 'Αθήνας (see below, p. 30, note 2).
The two-year archonship of Damasias and his violent ejection from office
(Aristot. *Respub. Ath.* c. 13), as also the request urged upon Solon to crown his
work by making himself tyrant, *i.e.* to become perpetual archon (Plut. *Sol.* 14)
— much as Pittacus of Mitylene had done, whose office as aesymnete Aristotle
(*Pol.* III. 14. 1285ª 31 ff.) calls an αἱρετὴ τυραννίς, — all testify to the great
power and importance of this office in these early times.

[1] Among the notable persons who held the office of archon between 660 and 500
B.C., we might name Miltiades the Philaïd, archon in 659 B.C.; Solon, probably
in 594 B.C., but possibly in 591 B.C.; Damasias, in 583–81 B.C. or 581–79 B.C.;
Miltiades (the hero of Marathon?), in 524 B.C.; Isagoras, in 508 B.C., bitter and
for a time successful rival of Cleisthenes for the control of the Athenian state
(Herod. V. 66, οὗτοι οἱ ἄνδρες ἐστασίασαν περὶ δυνάμιος). It is not certain that
Draco was archon (Aristot. *Respub. Ath.* c. 4); see below, note 4.

[2] Under Solon, the choice of archons was made by lot from forty previously
selected candidates (πρόκριτοι), ten from each tribe. Later there were probably
one hundred such candidates (not five hundred — see Kenyon, p. 60, note).
But choice by lot appears to have been suspended for many years (from 589 B.C.?),
and was resumed about 487 B.C. (Telesinus, archon). Cf. Aristot. *Respub. Ath.*
cc. 8, 22, and 13.

[3] On the significance of the choice of στρατηγοί, see Gilbert, *Beitr. zur innern
Gesch. Athens im Zeitalter d. Pelop. Krieges*, Leipzig, 1877, pp. 1–72; Beloch,
*Att. Politik seit Perikles*, 1884, *passim ;* list, pp. 289 ff. Headlam's contention
(*Election by Lot at Athens*, 1891, pp. 21 ff.), mainly on theoretical grounds, that
the elections of generals at Athens had no party significance whatever, is hardly
borne out by all the facts. The importance of the elections, however, from this
point of view, has doubtless been unduly magnified.

[4] Draco, Ol. 39 (B.C. 624–0): Tatian, *Or. ad Graec.* 63; Clem. Alex. *Strom.* I.
p. 366 Pott.; Suid. *s.v.* Δράκων. Eusebius (*Chron.* II. 90, 91) gives the year:
Armen. Vers. Abrahamic year 1395 = Ol. 39. 4 = 621 B.C., but Jerome 622 B.C.
Diod. Sic. IX. *Frag.* 17 places Draco 47 years before Solon; 7 is a sure number
(Tzetz. *Chil.* V. 350), and 47 can only be a mistake for 27: B.C. 594 + 27 = 621.

several measures meant to remove the increasing alienation of the rich and the poor, and the proposal of new constitutional forms, —in which, since the discovery of the Aristotle papyrus, one is tempted to see the real beginnings of Athenian Democracy,[1]—the laws are put on record and codified, as a safeguard for the people, who now are making themselves felt as a powerful element in the state. Factional quarrels[2] between prominent families, which in many instances are strengthened by foreign alliances, prevail in this period, and are at their bitterest. The families of the Lycomidae,[3]

---

Cf. Busolt, *G. G.* I. p. 510, note 4. Aristotle (*Respub. Ath.* c. 4) makes Aristaechmus, not Draco, archon at the time of the latter's legislation. Possibly Draco was chosen archon soon after proposing his reforms, to carry them into execution: Solon was appointed archon for a like purpose. The exactness of the dates ascribed to Draco is perhaps to be explained on the supposition that his name occurred in the archon-lists. Still, the view that Draco was archon, held by all modern historians—the ancients speak of him as νομοθέτης, etc.—seems to rest wholly upon the word θεσμοθετήσαντα in Paus. IX. 36. 8; since θεσμοθέται often means οἱ ἄρχοντες (Dem. LVII. 66), it was inferred that θεσμοθετήσας here meant ἄρχων γενόμενος (C. F. Hermann, *De Dracone: Ind. Schol. Gotting. 1849–1850*, p. 5, note 15). But this inference is not justifiable: θεσμοθετήσας is here merely a participial rendering of θεσμοὺς ἔθηκεν in Aristotle's *Respub. Ath.* c. 4; cf. τοὺς νόμους ἔθηκεν, Suid. *s.v.* Δράκων. The κατά τινας of Eusebius (Syncell. 403, 11) suggests that there was an ancient variation in the date assigned to Draco.

[1] B. Keil, *Berl. Philol. Wochenschrift*, 1891, No. 17, p. 520. "Die Rhetorik das vierten Jahrhunderts [hat] die Bedeutung Drakons völlig vernichtet und allen Ruhm auf den Volksmann Solon gehäuft," Diels, *Sitzungsb. d. Berl. Akad.* 1891, p. 392. Cf. Aristot. *Respub. Ath.* c. 4.

[2] Aristot. *Respub. Ath.* c. 13, οἱ δὲ τῇ πολιτείᾳ δυσχεραίνοντες ... ἔνιοι δὲ διὰ τὴν πρὸς ἀλλήλους φιλονικίαν.

[3] The ancestral home of the Lycomidae (shortened form of * Λυκομηδίδαι, Λυκομήδης being a family name) was Phlya (Plut. *Them.* 1; *C.I.A.* II. 1113 gives tribe, gens, and deme, ὅρος χωρίου προικὸς Ἱπποκλείᾳ Δημοχάρους Λευκονοιῶς Τ ὅσῳ πλείονος ἄξιον Κεκροπίδαις ὑπόκειται καὶ Λυκομίδαις καὶ Φλυεῦσι). It was from Phlya that the Myron came who conducted the formal prosecution of the Alcmeonidae after the affair of Cylon (Aristot. *Respub. Ath.* c. 1; Plut. *Sol.* 12). Busolt (*G. G.* I. p. 508) pointing out that Themistocles, a Lycomid, was charged with treason by Leobates, an Alcmeonid (Craterus, *Frag.* 3 in Müller, *F. H. G.* II. p. 619; Plut. *Them.* 23) remarks that the family feud would seem to have reached back into the seventh century B.C. Diels, however, finds significance in the fact that Phlya (like Eleusis) was a religious community, and the Lycomidae a distinctively priestly family; as a supporter of

the Philaïdae[1] (who were, or soon became, connected by marriage with Cypselus, despot of Corinth), the Alcmeonidae[2] (who later became allied by marriage with the tyrants of Sicyon), are prominent in these controversies and rivalries. It is safe to infer that the ancient and powerful family[3] to which Cylon belonged, himself the son-in-law of a foreign tyrant, was equally prominent, if the issue of the struggle between the adherents of Cylon and the powerful Alcmeonidae — the banishment of the latter from Athens — is to be taken as a criterion.

the ancient, simple religion of the people, outraged by the license of the free-thinking, high-born Alcmeonidae, who unhesitatingly violate the places deemed most holy by the common folk, the Lycomid Myron becomes the formal accuser of the family of the guilty (*l.c.*, p. 390).

[1] The honors received and the offices held by Philaïdae are evidence of the prominence of this family. Miltiades was archon in 664 B.C. and 659 B.C. (Paus. IV. 23. 10, and VIII. 39. 3); Hippocleides, archon in 566 B.C., had unsuccessfully contested, with Megacles and other prominent young Greeks, for the hand of Agariste, daughter of Cleisthenes of Sicyon; a descendant of the earlier Miltiades, Miltiades, the oecist (Herod. VI. 38) was a formidable rival of Peisistratus, who was glad to make a compromise with him (Herod. VI. 35, 36; Marcellinus *Thuc.* 7: cf. also Herod. VI. 103); Isagoras, champion of the oligarchic reactionaries after the final expulsion of the Peisistratidae (Herod. V. 66–73; Aristot. *Respub. Ath.* c. 20), was archon in 508 B.C. His election to the archontate at the same time that Cleisthenes was entrusted with the reorganisation of the state shows that a compromise was effected between the two rival parties. On the relationship of the family to the Cypselidae of Corinth, cf. Herod. VI. 128; Cypselus was the name of the father of Miltiades, the oecist of the Thracian Chersonese (Herod. VI. 35; cf. Töpffer, *Att. Gen.* pp. 279, 280).

[2] On the Alcmeonidae, see below, pp. 42–61, with the notes.

[3] Thuc. I. 126: Κύλων ... τῶν πάλαι εὐγενής τε καὶ δυνατός. This family, or at least the members of it who participated in the Cylonian attempt, went into exile and were excluded from the amnesty of Solon. It is probable that it early became extinct, though the name Κύλων recurs in a sepulchral inscription dating from the sixth century B.C. (*C.I.A.* I. 472; Roberts, *Greek Epigraphy*, p. 82; Kaibel, *Epigr. Graeca*, no. 9). The slab bearing this inscription was found near Liopesi, the ancient Paeania, and it has been suggested that the family of Cylon were Paeanians (Ross, *Arch. Aufs.* I. p. 214). May not the family, early leaving their ancient homes, have survived under a slightly different name, Γύλων for Κύλων? The Gylon of history, Demosthenes' maternal grandfather, belonged to the deme Cerameis (Aesch. *Ctes.* 171), but perhaps in the marriage of his daughter to Demosthenes the Paeanian, there was a renewal of ancient local associations. Gylon himself, like Cylon, sought for his own wife the daughter of a foreign prince. Still, the hypothesis that makes Demosthenes a descendant, or even a connexion of Cylon, is not without the gravest difficulties.

Meantime — the measures of Draco proving ineffectual — the discontent of the people increases; it is greatly aggravated by a long and losing war with Megara, and by economical disorders at home in which the peasant proprietor grows poorer and poorer at the expense of the capitalists enriched by trade. At last in the demoralization of social conditions a Solon appears, and by drastic measures rescues the state from ruin. By his reforms the rights of all parties are measurably secured and peace and concord are ultimately established.[1] The people, however, as over-against the nobility, the poor as over-against the rich, are constantly gaining in influence, and to such an extent that only a few years after Solon's archonship, the peasant and the artisan classes[2] secure a representation in the board of archons, if only for a short period.[3] And yet in the local factional disputes that follow, between the men of the Plain, the Shore, and the Up-

---

[1] Cf. Solon, *Frag.* 5, and the excerpts in Aristot. *Respub. Ath.* c. 12, in which *Frags.* 4, 34, and 36 appear in a fresh version, with new verses.

[2] Aristot. *Respub. Ath.* c. 13: τῷ δὲ πέμπτῳ [*sc.* ἔτει] μετὰ τὴν Σόλωνος ἀρχὴν ... καὶ πάλιν ἔτει πέμπτῳ ... μετὰ δὲ ταῦτα διὰ τῶν αὐτῶν χρόνων Δαμασίας αἱρεθεὶς ἄρχων ἔτη δύο καὶ δύο μῆνας ἦρξεν ἕως ἐξηλάθη βίᾳ τῆς ἀρχῆς. εἶτ' ἔδοξεν αὐτοῖς διὰ τὸ στασιάζειν ἄρχοντας ἑλέσθαι δέκα, πέντε μὲν εὐπατριδῶν, τρεῖς δὲ ἀ[π]οίκων, δύο δὲ δημιουργῶν, καὶ οὗτοι τὸν μετὰ Δαμασίαν ἦρξαν ἐνιαυτόν. The name of the peasant class in this passage is in dispute, — ἄποικοι or ἄγροικοι. In the Berlin fragment (Pap. No. 163, I[b] 8. ed. Diels) the word is unmistakably ἀποίκων. In Brit. Mus. Pap. No. 131, Col. 5, line 7, there is a gap (ἀ[ ]οίκων); Kenyon, following Dion. Hal. *Ant.* II. 8, and thinking he sees a trace of ρ, restores ἀγροίκων. But the fac-simile shows no clear trace of ρ; the gap, though wide, could easily have been filled, as in lines 9, 11, 12, etc., by a sprawling π, which indeed I fancy can be made out; the word ἀπό in l. 18 fills precisely the space available for the corresponding letters in ἀποίκων, l. 7. In Dion. Hal., accordingly, ἄγροικοι — which is his regular word for *plebeii* — must be a gloss on the unfamiliar ἄποικοι (*i.e. rustici*), used in contrast with ἀστοί. Similarly ἀγροιῶται in Hesych. *s.v.*, and in Plut. *Theseus* 25 γεωμόροι are glosses for ἄποικοι. The word ἄποικοι in this sense should not arouse suspicion. If ἡ κώμη ἀποικία οἰκίας ἐστί (Aristot. *Pol.* I. 2. 1252[b] 17), then οἱ κωμῆται, *i.e.* 'country folk,' *rustici*, might be regarded, for name-making purposes, as the ἄποικοι of the πόλις, which may be regarded as the great political οἰκία. (To be sure in Herondas I. 2, ἀγροικίης is a correction for ἀποικίης, but below, at 13, we have ἀποικέω.)

[3] This provision, viz., that the ἄποικοι (ἄγροικοι, γεωμόροι) and δημιουργοί should have a share in the archontate, may have continued in force for several years. Diels, *Abh. d. Berl. Akad.*, 1885, p. 19, note 1.

land,[1] the leaders are members of the old houses, and their aims
are hardly those of disinterested patriots.[2] The rise of Peisistratus
to supreme control is, however, a sufficient evidence of the power
of the populace, while his numerous reverses, brought about in great
part by the Alcmeonid Megacles, and his compromises with his enemies, show that the ancient families are not without their influence.

---

[1] Although the geographical subdivision of Attica into Pedion, Paralia, Diacria
(Mesogaea), appears to be as ancient as the time preceding the incorporation of
Eleusis (Philoch. *Frag.* 35), it yet seems probable that the local factions founded
thereon are post-Solonian in origin. Plutarch, our only authority for making
them pre-Solonian, is inconsistent with himself; in *Sol.* 13, in *Mor.* 805 D,
and 763 D, he represents them as pre-Solonian, and explains the choice of
Solon as archon as a compromise between the three parties. On the other
hand, in *Sol.* 29 he regards them as post-Solonian, here agreeing with Aristotle (*Respub. Ath.* c. 13) and Herodotus, who distinctly asserts that Peisistratus formed his party (I. 59, καταφρονήσας τὴν τυραννίδα ἤγειρε τρίτην
στάσιν). We have them after Solon: did they exist before? On this point
we can only make the general answer, that nothing in our accounts of pre-
Solonian conditions makes this probable; indeed, at the time of Cylon they
certainly did not exist (Thuc. I. 126, πανδημεὶ ἐκ τῶν ἀγρῶν), and the language of Herodotus tells against it. With Diels (*l.c.*, p. 20), we must suppose
Plutarch here guilty of dittography. The recently discovered *Respub. Ath.* (c. 2
*ad init.* compared with c. 5) explains the blunder. Plutarch finds in his authority
— which is, or is based upon, an abridged form of Aristot. *Respub. Ath.* — for the
time immediately following the Cylonian troubles and preceding that of Solon,
words to the effect: τὴν παλαιὰν αὖθις στάσιν ὑπὲρ τῆς πολιτείας ἐστασίαζον
(*Sol.* 13), which a glance at the original text of Aristotle would have shown him
referred only to the contest between the notables and the commons (στασιάσαι
τούς τε γνωρίμους καὶ τὸ πλῆθος). His explanation of this contest as that between
the local factions is thus wholly gratuitous. The whole passage, from ὅσας ἡ
χώρα to τοὺς ἑτέρους κρατήσας (*Sol.* 13) has the appearance of a misplaced gloss.
See below, p. 25, note 3.

For a discussion of the names of these parties, see Landwehr, *Philol.*, Suppl.-
Bd. V. (1884) pp. 154-7, and for some remarks about the Parali, cf. below, pp. 53
and 57, and notes.

[2] The leader of the Pediaei was Lycurgus, probably of the ancient family of the
Eteobutadae (Βουτάδαι ἔτυμοι, *C.I.A.* II. 1386; but the εὐγένεια of the orator
Lycurgus refers to moral qualities, not to nobility of birth — pseud. Plut.
*Vit. X. Or.* 842 D); that of the Diacrii was Peisistratus, afterward tyrant. A
Peisistratus was archon at the time of the ancient battle of Hysiae (B.C. 669?
Paus. II. 24. 7); and while we cannot establish an ancient family of Πεισι-
στρατίδαι, — as would W. Petersen, *Hist. Att. Gent.*, 1885, pp. 71 ff., 114; cf.
Töpffer, *l.c.*, p. 228, note, — it is at least certain that Peisistratus claimed descent
from the ancient stock of the Neleidae (Herod. V. 65); the supposition that he

Such, in barest outlines, were the political movements at home. Early in the seventh century B.C. it would seem that something of the spirit of foreign conquest was active in the subjugation and absorption into the Athenian state of the commonwealth of Eleusis.[1] Later on, but some time before Solon, the spirit of war, whatever its occasion, stirred up a prolonged and humiliating contest with Megara for the possession of Salamis.[2] Still later, commercial enterprise showed itself in an increasing trade,[3] both export and import, in which the ancient aristocracy did not disdain to engage.[4] Towards the close of the seventh century B.C., Athens attempted to gain a foothold in the Hellespont,[5] undoubtedly in order to ensure to herself some share of the import trade in corn from the shores of the Black Sea, which at that time appears to have become the monopoly of Megara.[6]

---

belonged to the γένος Philaïdae (Westermann in Pauly, *R. E.* V. 1646, quoted by Petersen, *l.c.*, p. 115) arose from the fact that his native place (Plut. *Sol.* 10; Plat. *Hipparch.* 228 B) was Philaïdae, *i.e.* the village that became the Cleisthenean δῆμος of that name. For the family of the Alcmeonidae, from which came Megacles, the leader of the Parali, see below, pp. 42 ff., and notes.

[1] On the lateness of the incorporation of Eleusis into the Athenian state, cf. Busolt, *G. G.* I. pp. 379, 419. In the Homeric Hymn to Demeter (not long after 700 B.C.; Kuno Francke, *De Hymn. in Cer. Hom. compositione, dictione, aetate,* 1881, p. 27) Eleusis is an independent city. Athens once established to the north, a conflict with her neighbor Megara was inevitable.

[2] A long and bitter war with Megara, which had for its result the surrender of Salamis, precedes the political activity of Solon : Justin, II. 7 (*i.e.* Ephorus : — prope usque interitum armis dimicatum fuerat), and Solon, *Frag.* 2 (τῶν Σαλαμι-ναφετῶν . . . χαλεπόν τ' αἶσχος). The war for the recovery of the island probably took place *after* Solon's legislation, and in one of its later stages Peisistratus took part in it. Cf. Niese, *Zur Geschichte Solons und seiner Zeit* (*Histor. Untersuch. A. Schäfer gewidmet,* Bonn, 1882), pp. 22 ff.; also below, p. 73, and note.

[3] On the beginning and growth of Athenian trade, see Busolt, *G. G.* I. pp. 500 ff., and below, p. 55, and notes. Solon, *Frag.* 13. 44 : ὁ μὲν κατὰ πόντον ἀλᾶται | ἐν νηυσὶν χρῄζων οἴκαδε κέρδος ἄγειν | ἰχθυοέντ', κ.τ.λ.

[4] According to Hermippus, quoted by Plut. *Sol.* 2, Solon himself was a trader (ὥρμησε νέος ὢν ἔτι πρὸς ἐμπορίαν), and we are also told that it was for the sake of χρηματισμός rather than πολυπειρία and ἱστορία that his travels were undertaken (Plut. *Sol.* 25 ff.; cf. Niese, *l.c.*, p. 8). Aristotle (*Respub. Ath.* c. 11) remarks of Solon, that after his legislation, ἀποδημίαν ἐποιήσατο κατ' ἐμπορίαν ἅμα καὶ θεωρίαν εἰς Αἴγυπτον.

[5] Herod. V. 94 and 95; Strabo XIII. 599. The date of the conquest of Sigeum was probably about 610 B.C. Cf. Busolt, *G. G.* I. p. 513; and Töpffer, *Quaest. Pisistr.* p. 107.

[6] H. Droysen, *Athen. u. d. Westen,* p. 41, and Busolt, *G. G.* I. p. 500.

## II.

### THE PROBLEM.

At some point of time within the period outlined above, not earlier than 636 b.c.[1] and not later than 594 b.c.,[2] occurred the episode of Cylon.[3]

Cylon, a young Athenian of high family, who has in 640 b.c. won a victory at Olympia, at the time of a subsequent Olympic festival, with the aid of youthful comrades and of troops furnished by his father-in-law Theagenes, tyrant of Megara, attempts to seize the Acropolis of Athens and make himself master of the city. The people, however, rise *en masse* against him, hurrying in from the country, and invest the Acropolis.[4] The siege lasts long; most of the besiegers withdraw, leaving matters in the charge of the nine archons.[5] According to the earlier and probably more authentic accounts, Cylon and his brother escape,[6] while the comrades left behind are sorely pressed :

---

[1] Not before 636 b.c., because this was the first Olympic year after Cylon had won his Olympic victory. Jul. Africanus *s.* Ol. λέ (b.c. 640; p. 13, Rutgers; *ap.* Euseb. *Chron.* I. 197, 19S): [Τ]ριακοστὴ πέμπτη. Σφαῖρος Λάκων στάδιον. [κ]αὶ δίαυλον Κύλων 'Αθηναῖος ὁ ἐπιθέμενος τυραννίδι.

[2] The episode of Cylon is distinctly pre-Solonian : to be sure, Herodotus (V. 71) says of it only ταῦτα πρὸ τῆς Πεισιστράτου ἡλικίης ἐγένετο, and Thucydides (I. 126), Κύλων . . . τῶν πάλαι. Solon's archon year was either 594/3 b.c. (Ol. 46. 3, Sosicrates *ap.* Diog. Laert. I. 2. 62, *i.e.* here probably Apollodorus — Diels, *Rhein. Mus.* 31, p. 21; cf. Clinton, *Fasti Hellen.* II. p. 298) or 591/0 b.c. (if the text of Aristot. *Respub. Ath.* c. 14 be correct — 31 years before Comeas, *i.e.* 660 + 31). Ad. Bauer (*Lit. u. Hist. Forsch. zu Aristot.* 'Αθ. Πολ., 1891, pp. 46, 47), who accepts b.c. 661/0 as Comeas's date (after Töpffer, *Quaest. Pisistr.* pp. 142 ff.), thinks that the δευτέρῳ in Aristotle (*l.c.*) is a copyist's mistake for τετάρτῳ, *i.e.* that δ' was taken to be 'two' instead of 'four'; the correction would yield (661 + 33) b.c. 594 as Solon's date, and thus confirm the Apollodorean tradition.

[3] The account given above is a condensed statement, only those items that bear on the date being emphasized.

[4] Thuc. I. 126: οἱ δ' 'Αθηναῖοι . . . ἐβοήθησάν τε πανδημεὶ ἐκ τῶν ἀγρῶν ἐπ' αὐτοὺς καὶ προσκαθεζόμενοι ἐπολιόρκουν.

[5] Thuc. I. 126: χρόνου δὲ ἐπιγιγνομένου οἱ 'Αθηναῖοι τρυχόμενοι τῇ προσεδρίᾳ ἀπῆλθον οἱ πολλοί, ἐπιτρέψαντες τοῖς ἐννέα ἄρχουσι τὴν φυλακὴν καὶ τὸ πᾶν αὐτοκράτορσι διαθεῖναι ᾗ ἂν ἄριστα διαγιγνώσκωσι.

[6] So Thuc. I. 126. But Herod. V. 71, in his briefer account, says nothing of escape; hence probably arose the erroneous statement of the later authorities.

some of them perish of starvation, and the survivors take refuge at the altar of Athena Polias. As the temple is in danger of pollution from the presence of dead bodies, the officers in charge, unquestionably the nine archons, promise the suppliants their lives and a formal trial, and lead them away. This promise is broken; while still under divine protection the suppliants are slain,[1] some at or near the altar of the Eumenides on the Areopagus, whither they had fled in terror, and others on their way thither.[2] The guilt of this sacrilege attaches to the Alcmeonidae, and in particular to Megacles, named in the later authorities as archon; the family of this man and its adherents are tainted by this crime, and not only for two generations, but for more than two centuries, remain under a curse.[3] The captured survivors of the party of Cylon are subsequently tried and banished.[4]

---

[1] According to Plut. *Sol.* 12, the Cylonians fastened a thread to the statue (of Athena), and held this as they descended; the thread broke, and Megacles and his fellow-archons attacked them. The breaking of the thread was doubtless the Alcmeonidean excuse for the sacrilege of slaying suppliants, it being taken as a sign that Athena had withdrawn her favor. This thread may be meant in the abbreviated form of the story in Schol. I. Ar. *Eq.* 445 (ἐξάψαντες τὴν ἱκετηρίαν· ἧς διαρρυείσης κ.τ.λ.).

[2] Thuc. I. 126.

[3] ἐναγεῖς, Thuc. I. 126, cf. 127, of Pericles; ἀλιτήριοι, Ar. *Eq.* 445 with Scholia, and often. For the conception among the Athenians, see Junghahn, *Agos-sühne bei Thuc. I. 126–139*, Berlin, 1890.

[4] This may be inferred from the language of the provisions of the amnesty-law of Solon (Plut. *Sol.* 19, ἄτιμων ὅσοι ἄτιμοι ἦσαν πρὶν ἢ Σόλωνα ἄρξαι, ἐπιτίμους εἶναι πλὴν ὅσοι ἐξ Ἀρείου πάγου ἢ ὅσοι ἐκ τῶν ἐφετῶν ἢ ἐκ πρυτανείου καταδικασθέντες ὑπὸ τῶν βασιλέων [*i.e.* presiding archons — βασιλῆς, one for each court?] ... ἐπὶ τυραννίδι ἔφευγον ὅτε ὁ θεσμὸς ἐφάνη ὅδε). The penalty of θάνατος, at least later fixed for one convicted in a δίκη τυραννίδος, was excluded by the terms of the compromise between the Cylonians and the archons (Thuc. I. 126, Herod. V. 71). Schömann thinks that the court was one held by the πρυτάνεις τῶν ναυκράρων (*Jahrb. f. Philol.* 111 [1875], p. 460), a doubtful hypothesis; see below, p. 32, note 2. Cf. Busolt, *G. G.* I. p. 408, note 1.

Stahl, who in *Rhein. Mus.* 46 (1891), p. 251, explains ἐκ πρυτανείου as referring to "das Archontengericht," withdraws this explanation, on p. 481, in view of what he supposes to be the meaning of Aristotle's *Respub. Ath.* cc. 3, 8, and explains this court to be the Areopagus. But this can hardly have been the case. The language of the amnesty-law distinguishes between the three courts (Areopagus, Ephetae, Archons), and ascribes decrees ἐπὶ τυραννίδι to the last. Again, the Σόλωνος θέντος of Aristot. *Respub. Ath.* c. 8, used of a regu-

Is it possible to date this event? The writers that have independently examined the available evidence have come to very diverse conclusions. Herodotus is the oldest authority for the statement that the event fell on an Olympic year. In the list of Olympic victors drawn up by Sextus Julius Africanus, and embodied by Eusebius in his *Chronicon*, Cylon is named as victor in the δίαυλος at Olympia in Ol. 35 (640 B.C.). This date, then, is the *terminus post quem*, while the fairly well established date of the archonship of Solon, B.C. 594, is the *terminus ante quem*.[1] The only years that would satisfy the conditions are, accordingly, B.C. 636, 632, 628, 624, 620, 616, 612, 608, 604, 600, 596. With the exception of B.C. 624 and the earlier dates, there is hardly one of the other years that has not found its advocates : thus, B.C. 620 has been claimed by Clinton,[2] C. Peter[3]; 616, by Duncker,[4] Hertzberg,[5] Holm[6]; 612, — a favorite date, — by Corsini,[7] W. Wachsmuth,[8] L. Ross,[9] Schömann,[10]

---

lation providing that the Areopagus should pass judgment upon conspirators against the state, shows that previously another court had taken action in such matters. In pre-Solonian times, there must have been much confusion of jurisdictions : Solon simplified the system of courts, regulating the competency of each.

The authenticity of Plutarch's quotation is attested by the fact that this ancient law was incorporated by Pythocleides in his amnesty-law, proposed B.C. 403 (Andoc. *Myst.* 78); it was so incorporated doubtless only as a venerable but largely otiose formula, since the judicial system involved in it had ceased to exist with Solon's reforms. It was in keeping with the spirit of the times, when the laws of Draco and Solon were revived as the main stay of the state (*C.I.A.* I. 61; Andoc. *ib.* 81, 82).

[1] For these dates, see above, p. 10, notes 1 and 2.

[2] Clinton, *Fasti Hellen. s. a.* (I. p. 206).

[3] C. Peter, *Griech. Zeittafeln*, p. 30, *s. a.*

[4] Duncker, *Gesch. d. Alterthums*, VI.[5] p. 96, note 2.

[5] Hertzberg, *Gesch. d. Griech. im Alterthum* (*Allg. Weltg.* II.) p. 106.

[6] Holm, *Gesch. Griechenlands*, I. p. 463 ("vielleicht um 616 v. Chr.").

[7] Corsini, *Fast. Att.* III. pp. 63-65. "Ol. XLII. Megacles Archon. Ergo quum Cylon Ol. XXXV. victor in Olympiis fuerit, ipsius facinus patriaeque occupandae consilium longe commodius ad Ol. XLII. quam ad XLV. revocabitur, qua Cylon ipse 60 aetatis annum superasset. . . . Ergo Cylonis facinus quod Olympiorum tempore patratum fuit adeoque Megaclis principatus ad ineuntem Ol. XLII. sive alteram ipsi proximam referri debet." The date 612 B.C. may be regarded as the vulgate date, and Corsini is doubtless responsible for it.

[8] W. Wachsmuth, *Hellen. Alterthumskunde*,[2] I. p. 470.

[9] L. Ross, *Arch. Aufs.* I. p. 215.

[10] Schömann, *Jahrb. f. Philol.* 111 (1875), p. 456.

Grote,[1] Duruy,[2] G. Gilbert,[3] W. Petersen [4]; 600, by Scaliger [5]; 599, by Boeckh.[6] Several writers leave the date uncertain : Curtius [7] thinks it fell between B.C. 612 and 596 ; H. Stein,[8] between B.C. 620 and 600 ; Landwehr,[9] before B.C. 612 ; E. Abbott,[10] not later than B.C. 612 ; Pöhlmann [11] is uncertain whether it was before or after Draco. Since the hint was thrown out by Niebuhr,[12] the first writer of prominence,[13] so far as I know, to urge that the episode of Cylon is to be placed at some date nearer 640 B.C. than 600 B.C., at B.C. 636, 632, 628, or 624 — *i.e.* before and not after Draco — is Busolt.[14] A re-examination of the evidence, and a consideration of a few points not hitherto noted, tend to confirm the correctness of this view.

The arguments upon which the claim for the earlier or pre-Draconian date is based are fourfold : (1) those drawn directly from the language of the best and most trustworthy sources ; (2) those drawn from a consideration of the probable age, at the time of the

---

[1] Grote, *Hist. Greece*, III. p. 88 (Harper ed.).

[2] Duruy, *Histoire des Grecs*, 1887, I. p. 378.

[3] G. Gilbert, *Handb. d. Griech. Staatsalt.* I. p. 128 ("um 612").

[4] Petersen, *Hist. Gent. Attic.* p. 79.

[5] Scaliger, 'Ολυμπιάδων ἀναγραφή, *s.* Ol. 45. 1 (Scheibel, p. 25, note 141).

[6] Boeckh, *Pind.* II. 1, p. 391 (" Megacles, Ol. 45. 2 archon fuit "); II. 2, pp. 301, 303. But see below, p. 51, note 1.

[7] Curtius, *Gesch. Griech.* I.[6] pp. 668, 669.

[8] Stein, Note on Herod. V. 71.

[9] Landwehr, *Philol.* Suppl.-Bd. V. (1884), p. 134.

[10] E. Abbott, *History of Greece*, I. pp. 292, 296.

[11] Pöhlmann, *Grundz. d. polit. Gesch. Griechenlands* (I. Müller, *Handb.* III.), p. 385, note 1.

[12] Niebuhr, *Vorträge über alte Geschichte*, I. (1847), p. 314, " das erstere [ἄγος Κυλώνειον] schon in die alte zeiten, in den Anfang der Olympiaden gehört." But as Niebuhr without hesitation puts Theagenes, Cylon's father-in-law, in Ol. 40 (*ib.* p. 331), his suggestion as to Cylon's date loses significance.

[13] Schömann, *Jahrb. f. Philol.* 111 (1875), p. 449, admitted that Herodotus's ἡλικιωτέων must mean youthful persons of the same age with Cylon, but did not draw the necessary inferences as to an earlier date than 612 B.C., which he accepted on p. 456.

[14] Busolt, *Griech. Gesch.* I. (1885) pp. 498, 505, with notes : the only argument distinctly urged by Busolt is that based on ἡλικιωτέων and ἐκόμησε, expressions to be used only of young persons ; he sustains this argument by a communication from H. Stein (*ib.* p. 505, note 2), on the probable meaning of these expressions in this passage. Of course, since the recovery of the *Respub. Ath.*, *i.e.* since January, 1891 — the earlier date for Cylon has been universally accepted (see p. 14).

affair, of the Megacles concerned, as also from a consideration of certain points in the history of the Alcmeonidae in these times; (3) those drawn from the probable date of Theagenes, Cylon's father-in-law. These considerations, it is believed, will be enough to create a strong presumption in favor of the date proposed. If, finally, after objections have been met, it can be further shown (4) that the adoption of this date, rather than a later one, will disclose something of a natural sequence and coherence in the movements of the time, as regards both the domestic and the foreign relations of Athens, this fact must be regarded as a confirmatory argument of no small force.

As preliminary, however, to the special discussion of the Date of Cylon, two matters call for brief treatment: first, the character and credibility of our primary sources of information on the subject, and, secondly, the nature and extent of the connexion of the Alcmeonidae with the affair of Cylon, — at least in so far as these two questions touch the problem before us.

## III.

### THE STORY OF CYLON: OUR SOURCES OF INFORMATION.

THE story of Cylon is first told by HERODOTUS (V. 71), very briefly, as an episode in his account of Cleisthenes of Athens, of Alcmeonid descent, in explanation of the reason why Cleisthenes was obliged to leave Athens as ἐναγής. It is again given, with fuller details and with interesting variations, by THUCYDIDES (I. 126), likewise as an episode, to account for the demand made by the Spartans, at the opening of the Peloponnesian war, for the banishment of Pericles who was also an Alcmeonid. The next author who we know told the story — there must have been others — was ARISTOTLE in his Athenian Commonwealth. It was probably given in full. In the copy of this work recently recovered, the early chapters have been lost, and we have references only to the last incidents — the trial of the Alcmeonidean faction, the casting of the bones of the guilty dead beyond the borders, the perpetual exile of the family, and the subsequent purification of the city by Epimenides of Crete.[1] All these state-

---

[1] Aristot. *Respub. Ath.* 1: καταγνωσθέντος δὲ τοῦ ἄγους [αὐτ]οὶ μὲν ἐκ τῶν τάφων ἐξεβλήθησαν, τὸ δὲ γένος αὐτῶν ἔφυγεν ἀειφυγίαν. 'Επιμενίδης δ' ὁ Κρὴς ἐπὶ

ments, which stand at the very beginning of the treatise as preserved, and are followed by μετὰ ταῦτα, preceded the account of Draco ; this fact makes it clear that Aristotle put before the time of the Draconian legislation, at least the affair of Cylon if not its consequences here touched upon. THEOPHRASTUS appears to have touched the event at least to the extent of asserting that it was the occasion of the dedication by Epimenides of two altars on the Areopagus, to Violence and to Pitilessness.[1]

The event is briefly referred to in the Excerpts from the Constitutions of HERACLEIDES ;[2] this account, based on a lost portion of

---

τούτοις ἐκάθηρε τὴν πόλιν. With Kirchhoff I read [αὐτ]οί for Kenyon's [νεκρ]οί, which is impossible because of the missing article. Diels proposes [ἐκεῖν]οι.

[1] Theophrastus appears to be, directly or indirectly (through Ister?), Cicero's authority in *De Legg.* II. II. 28, as also that of Clem. Alex. *Ad Gent.* 2. 26. See below, p. 67, note I.

[2] Commonly known as Heracleides Ponticus, and of late identified with Heracleides Lembos. The authorship of these Excerpts (the manuscripts usually begin with the words ἐκ τῶν Ἡρακλείδου περὶ πολιτείας Ἀθηναίων, but include also other πολιτεῖαι) is a matter of conjecture. Schneidewin (*Heraclidis politiarum quae extant*, 1847) showed that they could not have been composed by the philosopher Heracleides Ponticus, and demonstrated their dependence on Aristotle. Unger (*Rhein. Mus.* 38 (1883), p. 504) claims them for Heracleides Lembos (fl. under Ptolemy VI. Philometor — B.C. 180-145; Suid. *s.v.* Ἡρακλείδης Ὀξυριγχίτης, and, according to Diog. Laert. V. 694, from Calliatis in the Pontus), and in this has been followed by Busolt and others; but according to Rose (*Aristot. Fragm.*, p. 260) incorrectly. The author of these Excerpts would seem not to have been from Pontus, for [Aristot.] *Respub. Argiv.* (Rose, *Aristot. Frag.* 481; preserved in Orion, *Etym.* p. 118, 19), cites Heracleides Ponticus for a statement not found in the Excerpts. Rose claims that he was a pupil of Didymus drawing from his master : thus in [Aristot.] *Respub. Samior.* (Rose, *Aristot. Fragm.* 573; Schol. Ar. *Av.* 471 = Heracl. *Exc. Pol.* 33), Didymus — *i.e.* the original of the Scholiast — cites Aristotle by name, but Heracleides in his quotation from Didymus omits the name; see Rose, *Aristot. Pseudepigr.*, pp. 521, 532; also 479, 481. The frequent resemblances in phraseology between the Scholia (and certain Suidan glosses) and the Excerpts also suggest Didymus as the intermediate. Unger (*l.c.* p. 504) urges, that since with one unimportant exception — where Aristotle might have expressed two opinions — all the statements in the Heracleidean Excerpts coincide even verbally with what is extant of the Aristotelian Πολιτεῖαι, we must infer that Aristotle has been slavishly pirated (hence λέμβος); this is undoubtedly true, but it looks as if the material had come through a Didymean channel. Rose (*l.c.* p. 491) intimates that Didymus — *i.e.* the author of the original of the Excerpts — combined material from Ephorus with his extracts from the Aristotelian Πολιτεῖαι.

Aristot. *Respub. Ath.*, though very brief, furnishes one or two items not found in Herodotus or Thucydides : the name of Megacles as the leader of the party that slew the fleeing Cylonians is mentioned for the first time. The Scholiast on Aristoph. *Eq.* 445 gives three versions of the story in forms which show that Herodotus and Thucydides were the primary sources, together with some other writer on Attic history not to be identified : the items not given by Herodotus and Thucydides are, in the first version (Schol. I.), a κρίσις ἐν Ἀρείῳ πάγῳ (probably, as we find it nowhere else, a misunderstanding of the καθεζομένους δέ τινας καὶ ἐπὶ τῶν σεμνῶν θεῶν of Thucydides), and the mention of the fact that the Cylonians fastened to the throne of the goddess some token that they were suppliants, on the breaking of which they were stoned by the Athenians. The second and third versions (Schol. II., III.) are distinctly Thucydidean, and add nothing while they omit much (the κατέλαβε τὴν ἀκρόπολιν ὡς ἐπὶ τυραννίδι of Thucydides becomes ἐπελθὼν τῇ ἀκροπόλει λῃστεύει καὶ ἁλίσκεται). Pausanias three times mentions Cylon : once (I. 28. 1), in commenting upon a bronze statue of him seen on the acropolis of Athens, he expresses surprise that a statue should have been erected to one who attempted to make himself tyrant, and would explain it by the fact that Cylon was very handsome, as well as famous for his victory at Olympia in the δίαυλος and for his marriage with the daughter of Theagenes of Megara. Again, in I. 40. 1, he refers to this marriage alliance ; and in VII. 25. 3, speaking of the treatment received by suppliants at Athens, he says that the magistrates put to death the adherents of Cylon, suppliants of Athena, who had seized the acropolis, and that in consequence the murderers and their descendants were

---

It is, however, more likely that Aristotle himself furnished this material, obtaining it perhaps from Ephorus, or, what is more likely, from the same sources as Ephorus (and for that matter, the same as the βίοι of Satyrus, Sotion, and Hermippus), and that thus are to be explained coincidences of statement between the *Exc. Pol.* and the fragments of Ephorus, and what we know of the βιογράφοι named above, where some writers (Busolt, *G. G.* 1. p. 437) claim a non-Aristotelian origin for portions of the Excerpts. The close and perhaps exclusive dependence of the Heracl. *Exc. Pol.* on the Aristotelian Πολιτεῖαι can no longer be denied. Indeed, since the recovery of the *Respub. Ath.*, we may place yet greater confidence in them as giving us as far as they go — of course in a very much abridged form, occasionally in a different order, and with many corruptions — not a little of what was to be found in the Πολιτεῖαι.

ἐναγεῖς τῆς θεοῦ. DIOGENES LAERTIUS (I. 10. 110) briefly mentions the Κυλώνειον ἄγος, intimating that it was, in the opinion of some, the cause of the visit to Athens of the Cretan Epimenides, who, according to the chronological authority from whom Diogenes drew, came to Athens in Ol. 46 (B.C. 596-2). PLUTARCH (*Sol.* 12) gives a full account of the episode, with some additional details which are highly significant : Megacles the archon is mentioned as having promised the suppliants safety until trial ; on the breaking of the thread that connected the suppliants with the statue of the goddess, he and his fellow-archons attacked the Cylonians, stoning them, and butchering those that fled for refuge to the altars, sparing only such as appealed to the wives of their assailants : hence the Alcmeonidae were styled ἐναγεῖς and became objects of hatred. Afterward the survivors of the Cylonians, becoming strong, kept up for a long period an agitation against the family of Megacles. In due time, the quarrel being at its height and the people divided, Solon interposed with the leaders of the Athenians and persuaded the polluted Alcmeonidae to submit to a trial and to the decision of three hundred citizens. Myron of Phlya became their formal accuser, and they were found guilty ; the living were banished, and the bodies of the dead were cast forth beyond[1] the borders.[2] JULIUS AFRICANUS, quoted by Eusebius, furnishes us, as we have seen, the date of Cylon's victory at Olympia (Ol. 35, B.C. 640). Finally, SUIDAS, *s.vv.* Κυλώνειον ἄγος and Περικλῆς, has two glosses on the subject : he or his source blunderingly connects the event with Pericles, confounding him with the Μεγακλῆς of the original documents.[3] A

---

[1] This detail—the casting of the bones of the dead beyond the borders — cannot now be explained (Busolt, *G. G.* I. p. 508, note 2) as a mere dittography of the procedure in the case of the banishment of Cleisthenes (Thuc. I. 126 *ad fin.;* cf. Herod. V. 70, 72). Aristotle's language ([αὐτ]οὶ μέν Kirchhoff, [ἐκεῖν]οι μέν Diels) intimates that the guilt lay mainly with the dead; the ἐξορισμός of their bones was their punishment, and the family as tainted went into exile.

[2] Plutarch also accepts the connexion of Epimenides with the affair of Cylon. And the same is true of Cicero and Clement of Alexandria. See below, p. 67, note 1.

[3] Küster's suggestion, adopted by Bernhardy (*Suid. Lex., s.v.* Κυλώνειον ἄγος), that the original reading was οἱ πρὸ τοῦ Περικλέους, or οἱ πρόγονοι τοῦ Περικλέους, is shown to be unlikely (1) by the language of Suid. *s.v.* Περικλῆς, and (2) by that of the Heracl. *Exc. Pol.* 2, of which the gloss of Suidas (*s.v.* Κυλώνειον ἄγος) is virtually an abridgment (see next note).

fuller gloss is here condensed, with the omission of essential details : thus the suppliants are spoken of only as fleeing to the σεμναὶ θεαί, whereas in the fuller accounts they were suppliants of Athena, and fled to the σεμναὶ θεαί only as an incident in their efforts to escape.[1] Suidas adds the item, that, while opposition was made, Megacles (Περικλῆς) refused to be persuaded.[2] In still another gloss (*s.v.* Ἐπιμενίδης) of Suidas we read that Epimenides, born in Ol. 30, purified Athens of the Κυλώνειον ἄγος about Ol. 44, being then an old man.

The problem of the relation of these various accounts to each other, and to their sources which are now lost to us, is one that cannot be satisfactorily solved. But a few important considerations may be pointed out.

A chasm of several centuries seems to separate the earlier authorities from the later : are we, therefore, to remain satisfied with the meagre though vivid accounts of Herodotus and Thucydides and to look no further? Are all the new items given in the later writers to be viewed with suspicion, not alone such as contradict earlier statements, but also such as supplement them? Are we, with Symmachus, to assert that a statement is false because it does not occur in the narrative of Herodotus or of Thucydides?[3]

In the well-known passage at the opening of his history, Thucydides, seeking to justify himself for limiting his scope to the war between the Athenians and the Peloponnesians, remarks that the events preceding this war, both in the immediate and in the remoter past, are at once obscure and unimportant, — obscure and difficult of investigation through the long lapse of time, unimportant mainly

---

[1] Heracl. *Exc. Pol.* 2 (Rose, *Aristot. Fragm.* 611, p. 371). Τοὺς μετὰ Κύλωνος διὰ τὴν τυραννίδα ἐπὶ τὸν βωμὸν τῆς θεοῦ πεφευγότας οἱ περὶ Μεγακλέα ἀπέκτειναν. | Suid. *s.v.* Κυλώνειον ἄγος . . . Κύλωνος. ὃν καταφυγόντα ἐπὶ τὰς σεμνὰς θεὰς ἀποσπάσαντες αὐτὸν οἱ περὶ Περικλέα τὸν ᾿Αθηναῖον ἀπέκτειναν.

[2] Suid. *s.v.* : Περικλῆς . . . οἱ δὲ ἀντεπέτατον, Περικλῆς δὲ οὐκ εἴα πείθεσθαι. Here is probably a confusion arising from the words of Thuc. I. 127, οὐκ εἴα ὑπείκειν, where Pericles is mentioned as resisting the demands, not, to be sure, of Athenians, but of the Lacedaemonians. Cf. also Thuc. I. 135 : οἱ δὲ ᾿Αθηναῖοι . . . ἀντεπέταξαν.

[3] Schol. Ar. *Eq.* 84 : Σύμμαχος δέ φησι ψεύδεσθαι περὶ Θεμιστοκλέους · οὔτε γὰρ Ἡρόδοτος οὔτε Θουκυδίδης ἱστορεῖ.

from the point of view of military science, but also in all other respects. It thus happens that upon Attic history before the expulsion of the Peisistratidae he has very little to say;[1] he does not mention the great law-giver Solon, whose half-mythical figure dominates the following centuries,[2] nor does he name even Cleisthenes the reformer. Herodotus, the range of whose history is more extended, has occasion to treat more fully of early Attic history; but even he, when he passes beyond the generation preceding the Persian wars, has little to tell but piquant and untrustworthy anecdotes: his Solon is the friend of Croesus, and the traveller in Egypt; Solon's services to Athens as a reformer are dismissed with only a word.[3]  It would seem, then, that the Greeks of the fifth century B.C. had no clear historical impressions of much that preceded the times of Peisistratus. Later the case was different in some particulars.

In the narratives both of Herodotus and of Thucydides one episode of pre-Peisistratidean Athenian history stands out in unique prominence, — this episode of Cylon. This prominence is due to two causes: Cylon was the only person on record besides Peisistratus who had attempted by violence[4] to make himself tyrant of Athens; and, secondly, in the suppression of this attempt an important family had become tainted with sacrilege, receiving a stain that centuries of brilliant public service were powerless fully to wash away. The vividness and precision of the language of the two historians, and the fulness of detail given by Thucydides, are to be explained from the fact that in the traditions both of the Alcmeonidae and of their hereditary enemies the main features of the story had been handed down with singular definiteness and amplitude. Such vagueness as may be discovered in these accounts springs from the fact that both accounts are given incidentally, as episodes, and from the habit of these

---

[1] The language of Thuc. VI. 54 implies that uncertain stories were current in his day about the Peisistratidae.

[2] Niese, *Zur Gesch. Solons,* pp. 1, 2.

[3] As legislator, Herod. I. 29, II. 177 (see p. 53, note); as friend of Croesus, I. 29–33; author of a poem in honor of the despot Philocyprus, V. 113.

[4] Aristotle (*Respub. Ath.* c. 13) now teaches us that the prolonged archonship of Damasias was a usurpation of supreme power in the state. In Solon *Frag.* 32, τυραννίδος δὲ καὶ βίης ἀμειλίχου | οὐ καθηψάμην (cf. 33. 5, 6), an allusion to Damasias has been seen by Diels and Ad. Bauer.

historians in treating subjects of this sort, — apparently not from any uncertainty about the main points of the story.[1] The apparatus for the study of the earlier Athenian history used by the writers of the fifth century B.C. was not so extensive as that of their successors after the middle of the following century.[2] Not to attempt an exhaustive survey, it will be enough to call attention to a few leading names. Thucydides, whatever may be one's views as to the presence of personal bias in his writing, had certainly set the example of systematic research, although his enquiries were mainly confined to events of his own day. A vast amount of material was available, awaiting the scientific student: family, local, political, and religious traditions; records of ancient ordinances, of laws passed, and of legal decisions rendered, from before the time of Draco[3]; probably lists of officials, secular and religious; and a certain amount of literary compositions, as the poems of Solon. Hellanicus, the contemporary of Thucydides, in his four books on Attic history had used these recorded lists and inscriptions, but his work was inaccurate and provoked the criticism of Thucydides and of Ephorus.[4] The historians Ephorus and Theopompus, in the next century, had gathered a vast amount of material, and though their ideas as to historical evidence

---

[1] Is Thucydides (I. 126) correcting Herodotus (V. 71)? This is substantially the view of Wecklein (*Ber. Bayer. Akad.* 1873, pp. 33 ff.), and others, including Busolt (*G. G.* I. pp. 504, 505), who gives the bibliography. Schömann (*Jahrb. f. Philol.* 111 [1875], p. 452) controverts it, perhaps not wholly successfully. The answer to the question is determined by the meaning we give to Herodotus's πρυτάνιες τῶν ναυκράρων, on which see below, p. 30, and notes.

[2] On the studies in early Athenian history made by the Greeks, see Busolt, *G. G.* I. pp. 361–370, 436, 437, and his notes *passim.*

[3] According to Josephus (*Adv. Apion.* I. 4. 21), the laws were first put on record by Draco. Aristotle (*Respub. Ath.* c. 3) reports that the six θεσμοθέται were appointed — of course long before Draco, when the archontate became annual — to record the θέσμια; but see c. 41: ἡ ἐπὶ Δράκοντος ἐν ᾗ καὶ νόμους ἀνέγραψαν πρῶτον. The contrast is here suggested between mere records of legal decisions (θέσμια), and a formal code (θεσμοί, νόμοι).

[4] Thuc. I. 97. Ephorus, *ap.* Joseph. *Adv. Apion.* I. 3. 16: Ἔφορος . . . Ἑλλάνικον ἐν τοῖς πλείστοις ψευδόμενον ἐπιδείκνυσιν. Diels (*Rhein. Mus.* 31 [1876], p. 52) doubted whether Hellanicus reckoned by archons and treated of events as late as the close of the Peloponnesian war, but in this view he has been controverted by Wilamowitz, *Hermes* 11 (1876), p. 292, and Lipsius, *Leipz. Stud.* 4 (1881), p. 153.

were hardly such as would commend these authors to the modern historian, their writings formed the basis for subsequent writers. The material furnished by these different historians and by the earlier writers of *Atthides*, Aristotle and his immediate followers of the Peripatetic school seem to have put together, augmented by material independently collected, and subjected to critical examination.[1] The study of chronology, though not reduced to a science until the time of Eratosthenes,[2] had already begun in the compilation, for historical purposes, of lists of Olympic victors by Hippias[3] of Elis, later by Aristotle, by Timaeus[4] of Sicily, and others ; as also of victors at the Pythian games.[5] Critical lists of the Athenian archons were drawn up as early as the time of Demetrius of Phalerum[6] (B.C. 317-307 ; died B.C. 283), who compiled an ἀρχόντων ἀναγραφή and wrote περὶ τῆς Ἀθήνησι νομοθεσίας. It was not later than the middle of the fourth century B.C. that, following in part the example set by Hellanicus, there first appear writers of special histories of Attica (Ἀτθίδες), in which legends, history, topography, literature, religion, antiquities, were fully treated : as Cleidemus, Androtion, and above all Philo-

---

[1] Cicero, *De Fin.* V. 4: omnium fere civitatum ... ab Aristotele mores instituta disciplinas, a Theophrasto leges etiam cognovimus. Cf. Cic. *De Legg.* III. 6. 14. See, for the historical-antiquarian studies of the Peripatetics (Aristotle and his immediate pupils) which go mainly under the name of Aristotle's Πολιτεῖαι, V. Rose, *Aristot. Pseudepigraphus*, pp. 393-579, who, however, denies Aristotelian authorship, and Dümmler, *Rhein. Mus.* 42 (1887), pp. 179 ff. In the fragments of these Πολιτεῖαι, authorities are sometimes quoted and controverted, and this is especially true of the *Respub. Ath.* recently discovered. The problem of the sources of the latter work has not yet been solved; for some remarks on the subject, see Ad. Bauer, *l.c.*, pp. 37 ff., 155; F. Cauer, *Hat Aristoteles ... geschrieben*, etc., pp. 37 ff., and *The Nation*, May 7, 1891 (No. 1349, p. 383), etc. The independence of Aristotle has been emphasised by Oncken, *Staatslehre d. Aristoteles*, I. pp. 24, 25, and II. p. 330.

[2] On the chronological studies of Hellanicus and Eratosthenes, see Niese, *Hermes*, 23 (1888), pp. 81-102, and for Apollodorus, Diels, *Rhein. Mus.* 31 (1876), pp. 1-54 and Unger, *Philol.* 41 (1882), pp. 602 ff.    [3] Plut. *Num.* 1 *ad fin.*

[4] Suid. *s.v.* Τίμαιος ·. . . ἔγραψεν . . . Ὀλυμπιονίκας ἤτοι χρονικὰ πραξίδια.

[5] By Aristotle, or his pupils (Rose) : Diog. Laert. V. 126. Aristotle's Πυθιονῖκαι are cited in Plut. *Sol.* 11 and Schol. Pind. *Ol.* 2. 87.

[6] Demetrius Phalereus was a pupil of Theophrastus; cf. Diog. Laert. V. 5. 75, also I. 22, II. 7 (Müller, *F.H.G.* II. pp. 362 ff.). His archon-list was probably one of the authorities used by Apollodorus in preparing his chronological system: Diels, *l.c.*, pp. 28, 37.

chorus[1] (fl. 306 B.C.), who paid stricter attention than heretofore to chronology, narrating events in annalistic form at first according to kings, and afterward according to archons. Philochorus also made special studies of many historical subjects, such as the colonization of Salamis, Attic inscriptions, the Olympiads, and the like.

If we are to judge from the use made of it by subsequent writers, clearly the most important work produced in these times on the early history of Athens, especially from the point of view of constitutional changes, was the treatise on the Athenian Commonwealth (ἡ 'Αθηναίων πολιτεία,) ascribed by the ancients to Aristotle, and undoubtedly prepared, if not wholly by his own hand, with the assistance of some pupil acting as secretary, under his personal direction; it carries with it the weight of the master's authority.[2] The recent discovery of

---

[1] Suid. *s.v.* Φιλόχορος.  Cf. Boeckh, *Ueber den Plan der Atthis des Philochorus* 1832 (*Kl. Schr.* V. pp. 397 ff.).

[2] This treatise affords satisfactory internal evidence that it was composed a short time before Aristotle's death, between B.C. 326 and 323. We are compelled to believe, from many indications, that it was written mainly by Aristotle, with perhaps the help of a pupil who prepared certain of the less important passages, the padding, as it were; the work, since it everywhere bears evidence of the master's hand, was then revised, but not rewritten, by him. If we are ready to maintain — a proposition by no means self-evident — that the main body of the writings current as Aristotle's are the genuine works of the master in the original form, and that, accordingly, they are the only norm by which everything else is to be tested, we may still account for the "non-Aristotelian" peculiarities of the language of the *Respub. Ath.* as due, in part, to the fact that the historical sources (epigraphic and literary) are often given in verbal quotations, or at least in paraphrases that retain original forms of expressions; due in part, perhaps, to the stylistic idiosyncrasies of an assistant whose work was incorporated with the master's, and, finally, to the most significant fact that the work was intended not for the scientific inner circle, but for the "general reader," being, as it has been happily characterised by an English scholar, a sort of "primer of the constitutional history of Athens, and citizen's handbook."

Into the question whether the treatise is in spirit and method, un-Aristotelian, and whether it exhibits other features impossible in a work of Aristotle's, — carelessness and inaccuracy in historical research, radically inconsistent political judgments, etc. (cf. F. Cauer, *Hat Aristoteles die Schrift vom Staate der Athener geschrieben*, Stuttgart, 1891; Schvarcz, *Ungarische Revue*, April, 1891; Rühl, *Rhein. Mus.* 46 (1891), pp. 426–64, and several English scholars), — we cannot here enter. The evidence, internal and external, of essentially Aristotelian authorship as well as authority seems so overwhelming, that, as between the two alternatives,

this work in the writing on the *verso* of British Museum Papyrus No. CXXXI., and its publication by Mr. F. G. Kenyon, together with the attention given to it in current philological literature, and the promise on the part of eminent specialists of critical editions, render any detailed account of it unnecessary here. It is enough for our present purposes to remark that this important and authoritative work bears evidence of a discriminating use of earlier sources, sources at once extensive and various.

Of subsequent writers, who, drawing their knowledge from the authorities named above, doubtless dealt with the affair of Cylon, and were thus sources for the writers whose fragmentary statements have reached us, the names of some can be ascertained, while those of others have been lost. Thus Didymus Chalcenterus, contemporary of Cicero, besides being the source of most of the information on this subject given by the Scholiasts and in the lexicon of Suidas,[1] was the author of a work περὶ τῶν ἀξόνων Σόλωνος cited by Plutarch (*Sol.* 1), on the basis of which at least cc. 19–24 of the latter's Life of Solon were composed. Didymus drew from Aristotle's *Respub. Ath.*, and from the writers of *Atthides*, and must have drawn also from the treatise on Athenian νομοθεσία by Demetrius of Phalerum. Hermippus (fl. B.C. 230), pupil of Callimachus and writer of βίοι, — drawing from Aristotle and other writers, — was doubtless the most important immediate authority of Plutarch, supplemented by matter from elsewhere : it may have been he who compiled the statements about

---

one should prefer to modify his conceptions of Aristotle than reject this treatise. As Diels has pointedly phrased it (*Archiv f. Gesch. d. Philos.*, 4. p. 479, quoted by Gildersleeve, *Am. Journ. Philol.*, 12 (1891), p. 100), "Diese 'Αθηναίων πολιτεία [ist] nicht nur echt aristotelisch sondern aristotelischer als die meisten der uns erhaltenen Lehrbücher an welcher sich jene Skeptiker halten." For an argument aiming to show that Philochorus, writing about 306 B.C., knew and quoted the *Respub. Ath.* as Aristotle's, see my article in the *Am. Journ. Philol.*, 12 (1891), pp. 310–318.

[1] Didymus wrote extensive commentaries on Aristophanes. Cf. Mor. Schmidt, *Didymi Chalcenteri Fragm.*, 1854, especially pp. 246–61 and 261–99 (de Didymo interprete scenicorum poetarum scholiorumque principali fonte). Meiners (*Quaestiones ad Scholia Aristophanea Historica pertinentes : Diss. Halens.*, 11, pp. 217–403) aims to demonstrate "scholia historica [for Aristophanes] in universum . . . ex eodem fonte, Didymi commentario, fluxisse," and points out in detail the sources of Didymus for his statements. Rose (*Aristot. Pseudepigraphus*, pp. 400 ff.) sketches Didymus's relation to later learning.

Solon's political career and made the illustrative extracts from Solon's poems which we find in common in Plutarch and in a secondary version in Diogenes Laertius (I. 2).

Enough has been said to show that, though the fragmentary items of information that we possess about the affair of Cylon are found in writings of various kinds, which were composed several, and in some cases many centuries after Herodotus and Thucydides, they have the value of evidence much earlier, which is probably as trustworthy as that of the historians named. A tentative pedigree of these different parcels of information, showing as far as may be their relation to each other and to their probable sources, might be drawn up as follows : —

Herodotus and Thucydides are substantially independent, both basing their statements, probably, on distinct family and political traditions, and not on records. Aristotle, or at least the *Respub. Ath.* ascribed to him, is authority, certainly (1) for the statements about the trial of the Alcmeonidae and its results ; probably, (2) as we may infer from the language of the Heracleidean Excerpts, for some account of the murder of the Cylonians in which Megacles figured prominently ; and, perhaps, (3) for certain other statements made in Plutarch's narrative, which will be considered below. The sources, in turn, of the *Respub. Ath.* at this point of Athenian history, it is at present impracticable, if not impossible, to define with any certainty. The Scholia on Ar. *Eq.* 445, in the three versions, go back to Didymus, ultimately to Herodotus and Thucydides, and to some writer on Attic history whom we cannot certainly identify : in particular, Schol. II. and Schol. III. are Herodotean and Thucydidean ; while Schol. I., though briefer, has independent matter, which, partially agreeing with that given by Plutarch [1] and in the Heracleidean Excerpts, is doubtless taken from Aristotle's *Respub. Ath.*, combined with matter from some Atthid-writer (Philochorus?). Pausanias, in I. 28. 1, and 40. 1, was perhaps drawing from Polemon ;[2] in VII.

---

[1] Thus Schol. I. has λίθοις αὐτοὺς ἔβαλλον, and the thread (by implication, see p. 11, note 1), both of which details are not found elsewhere, except in Plut. *Sol.* 12. On the other hand it says εἰς τὴν κρίσιν κατέβησαν ἐν Ἀρείῳ πάγῳ instead of Plutarch's more correct ὡς ἐγένοντο περὶ τὰς σεμνὰς θεὰς καταβαίνοντες. It omits the archon's name and says nothing of the butchery of the Cylonians.

[2] If, as is more than probable, the statue of Cylon — see below, p. 41, note 2 — was an ἀνάθημα, it was doubtless commented upon by Polemon in his great work περὶ

25. 3, we have probably — at least ultimately — some Atthid-writer who bears a striking resemblance to one of the sources of Plutarch. The Epimenidean gloss of Suidas and the statement of Diogenes Laertius (I. 10. 110) cannot be traced to their final sources; the former, in part at least, seems to contain the tradition followed by Aristotle, as to the date of Epimenides's visit; the chronological datum in the latter is perhaps traceable to Apollodorus. The statements as to the dates of Epimenides are so contradictory, that for the present they may be left out of the enquiry.[1] Most of Plutarch's[2] statements on the affair of Cylon are traceable to Aristotle's *Respub. Ath.* A comparison of Plutarch's account of pre-Solonian affairs with that of Aristotle shows, however, first, that this dependence is not immediate,[3] and, secondly, that there is much admixture of foreign matter,

---

τῆς ἀκροπόλεως (Strabo IX. 396). This work seems to have been confined to ἀναθήματα, for Strabo adds τέτταρα βιβλία συνέγραψε περὶ τῶν ἀναθημάτων τῶν ἐν ἀκροπόλει. Pausanias made abundant use of it. Cf. Paus. V. 21, 1: ἐν ἀκροπόλει μὲν γὰρ τῇ 'Αθήνησιν οἵ τε ἀνδριάντες καὶ ὅποσα ἄλλα, τὰ πάντα ἐστὶν ὁμοίως ἀναθήματα. Kalkmann, *Pausan.* pp. 59 ff. and *passim.*

[1] See below, pp. 66-70, and notes.

[2] On Plutarch's sources in his *Life of Solon,* see Prinz, *De Sol. Plut. fontibus,* Bonn, 1867; Begemann, *Quaestiones Soloneae,* Göttingen, 1875. Cf. Meiners, *Diss. Hal.* XI. pp. 393, 394. In *Sol.,* cc. 19-24 are evidently from Didymus; perhaps also 17, 18 (first half), 25, 26, with quotations in 1, 11, 14, 15, 31, 32 (Begemann). C. 25 *ad init.* is distinctly Didymean (cf. Aristot. *Respub. Ath.* c. 7; Rose, *Aristot. Frag.* 39).

[3] At least the following passages in Plut. *Sol.* (chapter, page, line — Sintenis ed. Bibl. Teubn. 1877) bear resemblance to passages in Aristot. *Respub. Ath.* (chapter, page, line — Kenyon, 2d ed. 1891), and are evidently traceable to the latter work. Only once, however, is Aristotle here named (*Sol.* 25, *ad init.*).

| PLUT. *Sol.* | ARISTOT. *Respub. Ath.* | PLUT. *Sol.* | ARISTOT. *Respub. Ath.* |
|---|---|---|---|
| I., p. 154, ll. 28, 29. | V., p. 14, ll. 8, 9. | XV., p. 170. 14-31. | VI., p. 16. 1-19. |
| " " 155. 2, 3. | XVII., p. 45. 17. | XVI., p. 171. 1-3. | X., p. 28. 11-17. |
| XII., p. 165. 16-19. | I., p. 1. 1-p. 2. 2. | " " " 17, 18 | XII., p. 30. 3, 4. |
| " " " 24, 25. | " " 2. 3, 4. | (eleg.). | |
| XIII., p. 166. 21. | II., p. 2. 4, 5. | " " " 21, 22 | " " 32. 14, 15. |
| " " " 23-26. | XIII., p. 36. 1-6. | (eleg.). | |
| " " " 31-p. | II., p. 2. 3-p. 3. 12. | XVII., p. 171. 31, 32. | VII., p. 16. 21-p. 17. 1. |
| 167. 10. | | XVIII., p. 172. 14-17. | " " 17. 8-p. 20. 10. |
| XIV., p. 167. 22, 23. | V., p. 15. 10, 11. | " " " 26, 27. | IX., " 26. 4. |
| " " " 23, 24. | " " 13. 13. | " " " 28, 29. | " " 26. 10-p. 27. 1. |
| XV., p. 169. 21. | VI., p. 15. 15, 16. | " " " 31. | " " 26. 4, 5. |
| " " " 24. | " " " 14. | " " 173. 3-8 | XII., p. 28. 25-p. 29. 5. |
| " " " 28-31. | X., p. 27. 8-14. | (eleg.) | |

some of which came directly or indirectly from an Atthid-writer.
For the account of Cylon this writer may have been Philochorus;
for the narrative of the part taken by Epimenides it may have been
Theopompus, possibly Theophrastus, directly or through Ister: Plutarch appears to have been familiar with all of these writers, partially

| PLUT. *Sol.* | ARISTOT. *Respub. Ath.* | PLUT. *Sol.* | ARISTOT. *Respub. Ath.* |
|---|---|---|---|
| XVIII., p. 173. 10. | IX., p. 26. 1, 2. | XXIX., p. 185. 21-28. | XIII., p. 35. 9-p. |
| XIX., p. 173. 23-27. | VIII., p. 24. 5, 6. | | 36. 6. |
| "   "   " 28, 29. | "   "   " 7, 8. | XXX., p. 186. 30-p. | XIV., p. 37. 1-2. |
| XX., p. 174. 20-22. | "   " 25, 7-10. | 187. 2. | |
| XXV., p. 180. 16, 17. | VII., p. 17. 6, 7. | XXX., p. 187. 3-10. | "   " 38. 3, 4. |
| "   "   " 19, 20. | "   "   " 2. | "   "   " 18-21. | "   " "8-p. 39. 1. |
| "   "   " 25-29. | "   "   " 4, 5. | "   " 188. 5-8. | "   " 39. 1-5. |
| "   " 181. 10-24. | XI., p. 28. 3-11. | XXXI., p. 188. 25-27. | XVI., p. 44. 23-26. |
| XXIX., p. 185. 20, 21. | XIII., p. 33. 1. | XXXII., p. 189. 26, 27. | XIV., p. 38. 7, 8. |

A minute comparison of the wording of these parallel passages, and a consideration of the order in which they occur in the two writers, as also of extraneous
matter inserted and of important and illuminating facts omitted, show that Plutarch
was certainly not intimately acquainted with the *Respub. Ath.* The resemblances,
the dissimilarities, and the discrepancies alike are intelligible only on the supposition that Plutarch was transcribing from some work in which an abridgment of
these parts of the *Respub. Ath.* was embodied. In transcribing from this abridgment
he interpolates foreign matter, which is inconsistent with the unabridged Aristotle.
The abridgment omitted the main part of cc. 2-4, also c. 13 from p. 34, l. 1 to
p. 35, l. 9, as well as many minor statements. The poetical quotations of Plutarch
are from a different collection; such as coincide are in a different order. A reader
of the *Respub. Ath.* in its original form would probably not have said ἕκαστος
τῶν θεσμοθετῶν (*Sol.* 25), where the work reads οἱ δ᾽ ἐννέα ἄρχοντες, nor would he
have turned τὸ γὰρ ἀρχαῖον ἡ ἐν Ἀρείῳ πάγῳ βουλὴ ... ἐφ᾽ ἑκάστῃ τῶν ἀρχῶν ἐπ᾽
ἐνιαυτὸν [καθιστᾶ]σα ἀπέστελλεν (to be sure, the text is uncertain) into συστησάμε-
νος δὲ τὴν ἐν Ἀρείῳ πάγῳ βουλὴν ἐκ τῶν κατ᾽ ἐνιαυτὸν ἀρχόντων. He would not
have made Peisistratus active in the (earlier) Megarian war (*Sol.* 8); Aristotle had
declared this impossible from the point of view of the age of Peisistratus (c. 17).
At all events, if he had known that the *Respub. Ath.* had a contradictory statement, he would have inserted ὡς ἔνιοί φασιν as in *Sol.* 1 (cf. *Respub. Ath.* c. 17,
ληροῦσι οἱ φάσκοντες ἐρώμενον εἶναι Πεισίστρατον Σόλωνος). His ἔνιοι here, however,
is suggested by the language not of Aristotle, but of the common sources of Aristotle and his other authorities. If, as is probable, ὁ θεὸς Ἰαονίαν τὴν Σαλαμῖνα
προσηγόρευσε (*Sol.* 10) is traceable to πρεσβυτάτην ἐσορῶν γαῖαν Ἰαονίας (*Respub.
Ath.* 6), the connexion is altogether too vague for a first-hand contact. Especially instructive are *Sol.* cc. 18, 25, 30, when compared with the parallel passages.
     But the accurate delimitation of the relation of Plutarch to Aristotle is possible
only after a careful examination shall have been made of all the passages in the
*Lives* and *Morals* where the two are on common ground, and this cannot be here
undertaken. Incidentally one might suggest that Plutarch's otherwise unac-

at least at first hand.[1] All the channels through which Plutarch collected his varied information it is perhaps impossible to ascertain : certainly Hermippus and Didymus were concerned in the transmission, and perhaps Ister. The first of the Cylonian glosses of Suidas (*s.v.* Κυλώνειον ἄγος) has a marked resemblance to the item from the Heracleidean Excerpts (*i.e.* ultimately Aristotle's *Respub. Ath.*) ; while the other gloss (*s.v.* Περικλῆς), rewritten in the light of the former, has a Thucydidean foundation which is discernible in the Scholia cited : thus these glosses have characteristics that suggest Didymus as one of the intermediate channels. Finally, the chronological item in Julius Africanus is ultimately to be traced to one of the Ὀλυμπιονικῶν ἀναγραφαί made not long after the time of Aristotle, from the authentic inscriptions preserved at Olympia.[2]

---

countable omission in his *Them.* of the characteristic anecdote of Themistocles, Ephialtes, and the Areopagus (*Respub. Ath.* c. 25) may be explained on the hypothesis that the copy of Aristotle's work used by Plutarch did not contain this story. In *Pericles* 9 Aristotle is cited, but immediately there follow statements as to Pericles which directly contradict Aristotle (cf. Ad. Bauer, *l.c.*, p. 77, who believes, however, in a first-hand use of *Respub. Ath.* by Plutarch). It might be objected that Plutarch had the original copy, while ours (British Mus. Pap. No. 131) is an inflated and interpolated edition. I have tried to meet this objection, very briefly, in *Am. Journ. Philol.* 12 (1891), p. 317, note.

[1] Plutarch's *Theseus* is largely drawn from Philochorus. Gilbert, *Philol.* 33 (1874), pp. 46 ff., attempts to prove that Plutarch drew from Philochorus, not at first hand, but through Ister, who is the source of the whole Life except cc. 1, 2. Wellmann (*De Istro Callimachio*, pp. 31 ff.) has demonstrated an independent use of Philochorus by Plutarch, — in cc. 14, 16, 19, probably also in 24, 31, 35, 36, — as well as a second-hand use through Ister. Wilamowitz (*Phil. Unt.* I. p. 8) claims for Plutarch an immediate contact with Cleidemus as well as Philochorus. Theopompus was the ultimate authority of Diog. Laert. (*l.c.*) for a part, at least, of his account of Epimenides at Athens, which in some particulars agrees with that of Plutarch. Plutarch used Theopompus freely in *Lysander*, and elsewhere. On Theophrastus as a source (through Ister?), see below, p. 67, note 1.

[2] The inscriptions were recorded by the Hellanodicae, evidently immediately on the completion of the festival : Paus. VI. 8. 1 says of Euanoridas, γενόμενος δ' Ἑλλανοδίκης ἔγραψε καὶ οὗτος τὰ ὀνόματα ἐν Ὀλυμπίᾳ τῶν νενικηκότων (cf. Harpoc. *s.v.* Ἑλλανοδίκαι· . . . Ἀριστόδημός φησι, κ.τ.λ.; Rose, *Aristot. Frag.* 482). These evidently are the Elean records of Olympionicae mentioned by Pausanias (*e.g.* III. 21. 1; VI. 2. 3, and 13. 10). Rutgers, *Jul. Afric.* p. 1. Julius Africanus, in constructing his own list, probably made use, not of the original records, nor of Phlegon's list, but of a sort of chronological compendium apparently prepared by the Elean Aristodemus (fl. B.C. 150?). Cf. Unger, *Philol.* 41 (1882), p. 604. Gelzer, *Sextus Julius Africanus*, I., 1880, p. 168.

## IV.

### MEGACLES AS ARCHON.

UNTIL within a few years historians have had no serious difference of opinion as to the part taken by the Alcmeonidae in the affair of Cylon. The traditional account as given by Plutarch has been accepted as authentic, and the earlier statements have been interpreted in the light of it. But of late a difference of opinion has arisen, which it becomes necessary for us briefly to examine.

There are three possibilities as to the part played by the Alcmeonidae in the affair. The antagonists of Cylon, to whom the guilt of sacrilege became attached, may have been the officials who promised the Cylonians safety until the matter could be tried and then broke their promise : as such we might regard them either (1) as the whole body of officials, or (2) as a band headed by one or more of the officials. On the other hand, (3) these sacrilegious persons may have held no office whatever, but may have been a faction that ill brooked the restraint imposed by the officials, and attacked the party of Cylon while still under divine protection. In the first of the three possibilities we should be obliged (with W. Petersen) to consider all of the archons at this time as members of the family of the Alcmeonidae.[1] According to the second, substantially the traditional, view we should have to suppose an Alcmeonid (Megacles) prominent among the archons, to whose support the members of his family and their sympathizers rallied, — influential to such an extent as to carry with him some of his fellows in office in his efforts to punish the daring Cylonians even by unholy means. The third view, by which we are to consider the Alcmeonidae as an irresponsible and rival faction, is urged by Landwehr.[2]

The third explanation is inconsistent with the direct language of Thucydides and with the most probable meaning of Herodo-

---

[1] W. Petersen, *Hist. Gent. Attic.* p. 81.

[2] Landwehr, *Philol.* 46 (1886), p. 133. In *Philol.* Suppl.-Bd. V. p. 147, this writer argues that Cylon trusted to the Eupatrids to sustain him as against the ἄποικοι, and appeals to Plut. *Sol.* 14, where οἱ προϊστάμενοι (by him identified with the Eupatrids) urge Solon to make himself tyrant. He might also have cited one of the Thucydidean meanings of δυνατός, used of Cylon (I. 126), viz. aristocratic opponents of the people. But these are hardly sufficient grounds.

tus: in both of these writers the blame rests upon certain persons who give to the Cylonians a promise, which is broken. Herodotus calls these persons πρυτάνιες τῶν ναυκράρων. Thucydides, however, having said that the conduct of the siege had been committed to οἱ ἐννέα ἄρχοντες, adds, after an interval, that they,—οἱ τῶν Ἀθηναίων ἐπιτετραμμένοι τὴν φυλακήν,[1]—when they saw the Cylonians perishing in the temple, lifted them up from their suppliant position with a promise that they should receive no harm (ἐφ᾽ ᾧ μηδὲν κακὸν ποιήσουσι), led them off, and slew them (ἀγαγόντες ἀπέκτειναν). Herodotus asserts that the πρυτάνιες τῶν ναυκράρων lifted up the suppliants upon the promise that they should not be slain (ὑπεγγύους πλὴν θανάτου); the blame of the murder, however, he adds, is attached to the Alcmeonidae; he does not, it is true, distinctly identify, as does Thucydides, the murderers with those who gave the promise. This failure is to be most rationally explained it seems to me, from some such considerations as the following: Herodotus, for one reason or another,[2] has always a good word for the Alcmeonidae, and appears ready to explain away certain objectionable stories told of them. The affair of Cylon was an all-important episode in the traditions of the family. It seems to be highly probable that the family traditions preserved the fact[3] that at the time of the affair one of their number was chief official of the

---

[1] This statement of Thucydides is abbreviated in Schol. I. Ar. *Eq.* 445 into the unmeaning οἱ Ἀθηναῖοι.

[2] The glories of the family are celebrated in Herod. VI. 121–131, from Megacles, the father of Alcmeon, down to Pericles: the Alcmeonidae freed Athens far more than even Harmodius and Aristogeiton (VI. 123); it is unlikely that they were traitorously disposed toward Athens at the time of Marathon (VI. 115, 121). They are ἐναγέες (I. 61; cf. V. 70, 71); in exile because of Peisistratus (I. 64); later, while still in exile because of the Peisistratidae, after a defeat at Leipsydrium, they built the temple at Delphi (V. 62); at last they are restored to their home (V. 69–73), though afterward, about 490 B.C., they are under a cloud (Herod. VI. 115, and Pind. *Pyth.* 7. 15). The ostracism of Megacles III., nephew of Cleisthenes, as an upholder of the Peisistratidae, not long after the battle of Marathon, attested by Aristot. *Respub. Ath.* c. 22, is new evidence on this last point: see p. 46, note.

[3] The family tradition seems also to have been preserved by the writer who gives (*ap.* Plut. *Sol.* 12) the distinctly Alcmeonidean explanation and justification of the conduct of Megacles and his associates, viz. that the breaking of the thread which connected the suppliants with the statue of Athena implied that the goddess rejected such a relation. Grote, *Hist. Greece*, III. p. 83 and note.

state, holding the position of archon, one of the board of nine chief magistrates known collectively in the fifth century as οἱ ἄρχοντες, and that he was the head of an ardent faction.[1] There is good reason for maintaining that these nine officers were known at the time of the affair of Cylon, not as οἱ ἄρχοντες, but as οἱ πρυτάνεις (Ion. πρυτάνιες).[2]

---

[1] Herodotus mentions Athenian archons as such only once (VIII. 51. 5, Calliades, archon 480/79 B.C.), while Thucydides does frequently; thus Herodotus does not mention the fact that Solon was archon, nor Hippocleides, nor Isagoras, though he names the men, and though the election of the latter to the archonship in 508/7 B.C. was an indication of the success of his faction. The argument *a silentio* has very little weight when we are dealing with Herodotus's treatment of political history.

[2] It is highly probable that up to the time of Solon the nine higher magistrates were called πρυτάνεις, '*fore*men,' 'chiefs,' and that at their head stood the βασιλεύς. After Solon, under whom the board was more definitely organized and unified (Aristot. *Respub. Ath.* cc. 3, 8; Diog. Laert. I. 2. 58, quoting Apollodorus, who probably here drew from Demetr. Phal. περὶ νομοθεσίας), and the precedence of the ἄρχων over the βασιλεύς had become an established fact, the whole board received the name of οἱ ἐννέα ἄρχοντες. The term πρυτάνεις was thereupon technically appropriated by the chiefs of the naucraries, and continued to be so used until the time of Cleisthenes. Later, when the naucraries had ceased to exist in their ancient form, the term passed over to the chiefs, for the time being, of the newly organized Senate, acquiring the sense in which the word is most familiar to the student of Athenian history.

The arguments urged in support of the proposition that the pre-Solonian archons were called πρυτάνεις may be summed up (mainly after Busolt) as follows: (1) in post-Solonian times the fees of the archons' courts were called πρυτανεῖα, a use of language that cannot be explained except as a survival from pre-Solonian times. (2) In the amnesty-law of Solon (Plut. *Sol.* 19), three courts are mentioned: that of the Areopagus, that of the Ephetae, and that ἐκ πρυτανείου (see above, p. 11, note 4). From Aristot. *Respub. Ath.* c. 3, pp. 6, 7 (hitherto known only in *Lex. Seguer.* p. 449, 17 = Suid. *s.v.* ἄρχοντες οἱ ἐννέα τίνες) we learn that the so-called archons held courts; hence ἐκ πρυτανείου (= ἐκ τοῦ πρυτάνεως, *i.e.* the later archon, if not ἐκ τῶν πρυτάνεων : Plut. *Sol.* 19 *ad fin.* explains by πρυτάνεις; cf. Schömann, *ib.* p. 460) in this law must have referred to the archon's court, if not to the archons' court. The original language of Aristotle, now happily recovered, does not justify us in maintaining that the archons might not, under certain circumstances, pass and execute judgment collectively, though they commonly exercised independent jurisdiction. Cf. Meier and Schömann, *Att. Proc.* I. p. 15, note 21 (Lipsius). (3) Thuc. (I. 126) informs us that the — so-called — archons had supreme direction of the state in the time of Cylon (τότε). The ancient home and headquarters of the government (τὰς ἀρχὰς ... πρυτανεῖον, Thuc. II. 15) was the Prytaneum. (4) In many Asiatic Ionian colonies a πρύτανις followed the

Now the tradition also handed down the fact that πρυτάνεις made and broke the promise to the Cylonians. Herodotus, we are to suppose, was not aware of the identity of the πρυτάνεις and what in his day were called ἄρχοντες : he held them to be different officials ; hence, on hearing or reading that the πρυτάνεις were the responsible persons, and knowing that the Alcmeonidae, one or more of them, were ἄρχοντες at the time, he inferred that the blame for the murder of the Cylonians was wrongly attached to the Alcmeonidae. The only πρυτάνεις in Attic history that he knew about were the πρυτάνεις τῶν ναυκράρων : hence he very naturally wrote πρυτάνεις τῶν ναυκράρων, inferring that these officials were the guilty party, not the Alcmeonidean ἄρχοντες.[1] Had he known that πρυτάνεις was but the pre-Solonian

---

βασιλεύς (Herod. I. 147), and the chief official for a long time afterward continued to retain this designation; *e.g.* in Miletus (Aristot. *Pol.* VIII. (V.) 4. 5, p. 1305ᵃ 18), Ephesus (*C.I.G.* 2955), etc. The expression πρύτανις is often used for βασιλεύς (Blass, *Hermes,* 13 [1878], p. 386). The chief official would thus be known both as βασιλεύς and as πρύτανις. Of Epaenetus, Attic archon in B.C. 636, pseud.-Hippys of Rhegium (Müller, *F. H. G.* II. p. 14) wrote ἐπὶ βασιλέως Ἐπαινέτου. (5) Suid. *s.v.* πρύτανις . . . βασιλεύς, ἄρχων, κ.τ.λ., is probably too vague to be in evidence for the practice in Athens. On the whole subject, cf. Busolt, *G. G.* I. pp. 408, 409.

The recently discovered *Respub. Ath.* does not seem, on first examination, distinctly to bear out this theory, though there is nothing in the treatise that tells decidedly against it except that, if the theory be correct, we must admit that Aristotle was unacquainted with the facts. One or two arguments, however, are suggested from the historical conditions set forth in the work itself: viz. (6) the archon's official residence, or "office," was the Prytaneum (c. 3); the Polemarch's, — anciently, — the Polemarcheum; that of the Thesmothetae, the Thesmotheteum. As the name of the officer in the two latter cases suggested that of the place of his activity, so in the former, Prytaneum must have arisen from πρύτανις (= ἄρχων). (7) In c. 4 occur these words : τοὺς μὲν ἐννέα ἄρχοντας . . . στρατηγοὺς δὲ καὶ ἱππάρχους . . . τοὺς πρυτάνεις καὶ τοὺς στρατηγοὺς καὶ τοὺς ἱππάρχους. The text as it stands is corrupt, and the point must not be pressed; but does not this collocation suggest that, in the source, at least, of this passage, τοὺς πρυτάνεις and τοὺς ἐννέα ἄρχοντας were identical in meaning? Later on in the work, of course, πρυτάνεις is used in its fifth century sense (cc. 29, 43).

[1] Aristot. *Respub. Ath.* c. 8 seems to show that the institution of the ναυκραρίαι. was pre-Solonian, though the reorganization of the system is distinctly Solonian. Hence Gilbert's contention (*Jahrb. f. Philol.* 111 [1875], pp. 9–20) that both the institution and the name begin with Solon (Phot. *s.v.* ναυκραρία) is futile. Schömann (*Jahrb. f. Philol.* 111 [1875], p. 454) and others — see Busolt, *G. G.*

name for the ἄρχοντες, such an inference would not have been made, and the passage in Herodotus would then have perfectly agreed with that of Thucydides,[1] as also with the statements of the other writer or

---

I. p. 502 — maintain that the ναυκραρίαι were established toward the end of the seventh century B.C., *i.e.* a short time before Solon, to extend the Attic navy and to protect the newly developing merchant marine; Solon merely gives the institution a more definite organization. Schömann's conclusions are doubtless sound, though his argument from the use of ἐκ πρυτανείου (*ib.* p. 460; cf. *Attischer Process*, I. p. 25 [Lipsius]) may be unsatisfactory.

[1] The language of Herodotus is, on the face of it, difficult to reconcile with that of Thucydides: the former puts the blame on one set of officials, the latter on another. There are several ways of accounting for this difference; the one suggested above seems to me on the whole the most probable. We might (A) regard the passage in Herodotus as textually unsound, *i.e.* that τῶν ναυκράρων is an interpolation. But the source of Harpocration *s.v.* ναυκραρικά evidently had a text with τῶν ναυκράρων, as is shown by the attempt to explain the word as equivalent to ἄρχοντες (ναυκράρους γὰρ τὸ παλαιὸν τοὺς ἄρχοντας ἔλεγον ὡς καὶ ἐν τῇ ἑ Ἡροδότου δηλοῖ). Accepting the text, then, as substantially sound, we may (B) explain the language in one of three ways: either (*a*), as does Harpoc. *s.v.* ναυκραρικά, by taking ναύκραροι as another name for 'archon.' This is extremely improbable, when we regard the meanings given to the word, and the history and nature of the institution of naucraries. This explanation is undoubtedly merely an attempt to reconcile the language of Herodotus with that of Thucydides. It is interesting as perhaps an early — Didymean? — attempt. Or (*b*) we may hold that Herodotus is giving the actual facts in the case, *i.e.* that certain officials known as prytans of the naucraries did have a part, and a very responsible part, in the Cylonian sacrilege. This again may be taken in one of two ways: either (*a*) there is no essential contradiction between Herodotus and Thucydides; there were two sets of officials concerned, the prytans of the naucraries and the archons; the former may be regarded either (*a′*) as executive officers acting under the order of their superiors, or (*β′*) the local leaders (ναυκράρους = δημάρχους) who came with their people ἐκ τῶν ἀγρῶν and subsequently handed over the conduct of affairs to the archons: Herodotus — following Alcmeonidean tradition — emphasizes the part taken by the prytans; Thucydides, that of the archons. Thucydides thinks Herodotus mistaken, and corrects him. Or (β) we may hold that there were two accounts of the affair, one of which made the archons responsible, — followed by Thucydides, and the other the prytans of the naucraries, — followed by Herodotus. Or finally (*c*) we may explain the matter as given above, viz. that we have here not an exact statement of the facts (τῶν ναυκράρων), but only a partially exact statement (πρυτάνιες), vitiated by the addition, made with honest intent, of an explanation (τῶν ναυκράρων) which, though supposed to throw light on the matter, thoroughly darkens it. We have thus to do with a mental interpolation on the part of Herodotus.

writers from whom Plutarch and Pausanias drew. In the light of these considerations, to suppose the Alcmeonidae to have had no connexion whatever, as officials, with the Cylonian affair is distinctly to discredit the most obvious meaning of our best sources, and is an arbitrary procedure for which there is no sufficient justification.[1]

If, now, the Alcmeonidae were officials at the time, it remains to be determined whether the whole body of archons was made up of Alcmeonidae, or whether only the leading archon was an Alcmeonid supported by his family and friends. The objections to the former view are mainly *a priori*. It seems quite unlikely that one family should have gained such power in Athens at this time of factional and family feuds as to obtain possession of all of the archonships. Not many years later we find that competition for these offices is so strong that candidates are elected even outside of the privileged class, and that a compromise is effected by which each of the three classes shall be duly represented. Again: the Cylonians received a promise of trial; the court before which the survivors were tried — and by which they were condemned to exile, the penalty of death having been made impossible by the promise of the officials — was undoubtedly that of the Prytaneium. This court was distinctly the archon's court, if not — as is more likely — the court of the college of archons.[2] Acting together in promising a fair trial, the archons would have sat together in judgment. Now it is extremely improbable that the judges of the survivors in this cause could have been none other than the murderers of the friends of the survivors; it is therefore next to impossible that all of the archons could have been Alc-

---

Of the possible explanations summarized above, A is clearly most improbable; B *a* is likewise improbable; B *b* a (a', β') and β have each their advocates, whom we need not here enumerate. The greater probability of B *c* must be judged from the available evidence, which, so far as I know, is here presented in full in the text, or in the notes, though very briefly.

If the conclusion B *c* be correct, the prytans of the naucraries disappear wholly from the scene of the Cylonian affair, and all inferences as to their duties and functions, based on their supposed connexion with it, lose their foundation. In all its essential features, the story as given in our various accounts now becomes clear, and thoroughly consistent with itself.

[1] For an additional, though hardly probable argument, based on the presence of a statue of Cylon in the acropolis, see below, p. 41, note 2.

[2] See above, p. 11, note 4, and p. 30, note 2.

meonidae, though not at all unlikely that one or more of them may have belonged to the family.

Having now shown that one or more of the Alcmeonidae were connected, as officials, with the suppression of the Cylonian attempt, and tainted by the sacrilege involved not only in the murder of suppliants before Athena, but also in the violation of a solemn promise, let us briefly examine the evidence that tends to show that Megacles the Alcmeonid was archon at the time of the affair.

The first appearance[1] of the name Megacles is in the Heracleidean Excerpts (οἱ μετὰ Μεγακλέους). The dependence of these Excerpts upon Aristotle's *Respub. Ath.* has been too often proved to require demonstration here.[2] There is, therefore, a strong presumption in favor of the view that in the introductory account in the *Respub. Ath.* mention was made of Megacles, if not as an archon, at least as the leader of the anti-Cylonian party. This presumption is made more certain when we bear in mind the thorough familiarity with the family of the Alcmeonidae apparent in this treatise, as well as the nature of the information given in the earlier or historical portion of it (cc. 1–41). Here several members of the family are not only mentioned, but mentioned in such a way as to show that the writer, or at all events his authorities, had them distinctly differentiated in mind. The first person named in this treatise with his parentage affixed is Megacles, son of Alcmeon, the leader of the Parali (c. 13); this statement about the parentage, not made in the case of his rivals, would seem to show one of two things, if not both : either that the father Alcmeon had been mentioned in an earlier portion of the account, or that a Megacles had been mentioned earlier, from whom the later Megacles (his grandson) was to be distinguished by the addition of his father's name. The adoption of the latter alternative confirms us in our contention that the Megacles of the affair of Cylon was named in the *Respub. Ath.;* the adoption of the former would add another bit of evidence in proof of the statement that the Alcmeonidae figured largely in this work.[3]

---

[1] The absence of the name in Herodotus and Thucydides need not awaken suspicion; the important thing in the story, told only as an episode, is the family taint, not the guilt of the original offender. As we have noted already, even Thucydides does not mention such memorable names as Solon and Cleisthenes.

[2] See above, p. 15, note 2.

[3] Perhaps Aristotle was here merely transcribing Herodotus's Μεγακλέος τοῦ

That Megacles was named in the *Respub. Ath.* can hardly be
disputed; but that there was a distinct statement in the same
work that he was archon is not capable of demonstration. This
is, however, extremely probable, since archons are again and again
mentioned by name in the treatise, the oldest being Aristaechmus, in
whose archonship the reforms of Draco were proposed (c. 4). The
absence of such an assertion in the Heracleidean Excerpts and in the
glosses of Suidas means nothing; all these statements are abridgments
of abridgments, and it was perhaps regarded as unnecessary to retain
an item which would be taken for granted. The presence of this
statement in Plutarch — and, by inference, in the work from which
Pausanias drew — would show simply that Plutarch had some authority for it, not necessarily that of the *Respub. Ath.;* for, though we
may hold that much in Plutarch is traceable to this work, most of it
seems to have come so indirectly and with so much admixture of other
material, that it is hazardous to quote Plutarch, when unsupported,
as authority for Aristotle. That, however, Plutarch did draw from
some good authority in which the statement was made that Megacles
was archon, is more than probable; the concurrence, together with
the essential independence, of the items given in Schol. I. Ar. *Eq.*
445, in Paus. VII. 25. 3, in Suidas *s.vv.* Κυλώνειον ἄγος and Περικλῆς,
and in Plut. *Sol.* 12, point to some writer or writers of a good period,
possibly only Aristotle,[1] but probably also an Atthid-writer, by whom

---

Ἀλκμέωνος (I. 59). Still, even on this supposition, it is significant that he did not
also transcribe Ἀριστολαΐδεω with Λυκούργου. The Alcmeonidae interested him.
Other instances, in the *Respub. Ath.*, of mentions of parentage are: Aristeides
(son of Lysimachus, cc. 22, 23); Cimon (Miltiades, c. 26); Cleon (Cleaenetus,
c. 28); Ephialtes (Sophonides, c. 25); Hipparchus (Charmus, c. 22); Isagoras
(Teisander, c. 20); Megacles (Hippocrates, c. 22); Themistocles (Neocles, c.
23); Theramenes (Hagnon, c. 28); Xanthippus (Ariphron, c. 22). Probably
also Pythodorus (c. 29); following Diog. Laert. IX. 8. 54, I proposed το[ῦ
Πολυ(ζή]λου (*Nation*, No. 1349, p. 384), but now adopt the Ἐπι(ζή]λου of Kaibel-
Wilamowitz, who refer to *Athen. Mittheil.* 14 (1889), p. 398.

[1] That Aristotle could hardly have been the only writer from whom Plutarch
drew is shown by the language of Pausanias (VII. 25. 3), which, as the context
shows, though dealing with the same subject, treats it after the fashion of an
Atthid-writer, and is thus probably drawn from an Atthid-writer (through Polemon or Ister?) : Philochorus was the favorite source for these later writers. It is,
however, not impossible that the Aristotelian element in Plutarch's account of the

the fact that Megacles was archon was distinctly expressed. From
Plutarch's well-known partiality for Philochorus, who we know treated
Attic history according to archons,[1] it is perhaps safe to infer that
this famous writer, in the third book of whose *Atthis* the affair of Cylon was doubtless mentioned, was the source that we desire. At all
events, we have fourth century B.C. evidence (Aristotle's *Respub. Ath.*)
for the name of Megacles as that of the leader in the anti-Cylonian
movement; we have fifth century B.C. evidence (Thucydides) that
the archons, in part at least, were of the anti-Cylonian faction; we
have the earliest possible evidence (Herodotus, though apparently
not the much earlier Solonian amnesty-law) that the Alcmeonidae were
held responsible and punished for the Cylonian sacrilege. In the light
of this evidence, is it not safe to assume that at the time of the Cylonian attempt Megacles was one of the prominent officials, probably
the archon *par excellence ?*

affair of Cylon (though probably not of Solon's activity) may have reached Plutarch through Philochorus. A fairly clear case of such transmission is found in
Plut. *Them.* 10: cf. my article in *Am. Journ. Philol.* 12 (1891), pp. 313 ff.

[1] Cf. Schol. Luc. *Tim.* 30 (pp. 47, 48 Jacobitz): ἐπέστη δὲ (Κλέων) καὶ τῇ πρὸς
Λακεδαιμονίους εἰρήνῃ ὡς Φιλόχορος, π ρ ο σ θ ε ὶ ς ἄρχοντα Εὔθυνον, καὶ Ἀριστοτέλης.
Suid. *s.v.* ἔγραψεν Ἀτθίδος βιβλία ιζ´· περιέχει δὲ τὰς Ἀθηναίων πράξεις καὶ
<τοὺς> βασιλεῖς καὶ ἄρχοντας ἕως Ἀντιόχου τοῦ τελευταίου. Cf. also Müller,
*F.H.G.* I. *Frag.* 97 (Schol. Ar. *Pac.* 605), ἐπὶ Πυθοδώρου (Mss. Θεοδώρου); 108
(Schol. Ar. *Pac.* 466), ἐπὶ Ἀλκαίου (Mss. Ἀλκμαίωνος); 107 (Schol. Ar. *Vesp.*
210), ἐπὶ Ἰσάρχου, etc. On the annalistic form adopted by the Atthid-writers, see
Dion. Hal. *Ant.* I. 8; also Usener, *Jahrb. f. Philol.* 103 (1871), pp. 311 ff., and
Busolt, *G. G.* I. p. 363, note 4. Didymus made abundant use of Philochorus; cf.
Meiners, *Diss. Halen.* 11. pp. 336–72, who demonstrates more than two dozen
citations in the historical Scholia on Aristophanes. Marcellinus *Thuc.* 32, and
Harpocration *s.v.* περίστοιχοι also give us Didymean citations from Philochorus.
Possibly in the otherwise unknown Φιλοκλέους τινός, cited by Plutarch (*Sol.* 1)
as quoted by Didymus, we are to see an ancient corruption of Φιλοχόρου.

## V.

### CYLON A YOUNG MAN.

THE more important arguments upon which the claim for an early date for Cylon is based, drawn from the direct language of the sources, are concerned with the age of Cylon at the time of his attempt to possess the acropolis.

The earliest and in fact the only writer who gives any information on this point is Herodotus (V. 71), in these words : οὗτος ἐπὶ τυραννίδι ἐκόμησε, προσποιησάμενος δὲ ἑταιρηίην τῶν ἡλικιωτέων, καταλαβεῖν τὴν ἀκρόπολιν ἐπειρήθη. The word of especial significance in this passage is ἡλικιῶται, which though not found elsewhere in Herodotus is a word of good classical usage. It means ʻ age-mates,ʼ ʻ persons of the same age,ʼ but as actually used it seems to be restricted almost wholly to the young and to the old.[1] When used of combinations for political purposes, it can have reference only to leagues of youthful comrades and associates. There would be a manifest absurdity in supposing that a combination of middle-aged men was here meant ; the fact of age is not dwelt upon in speaking of men in middle life : this is a feature that impresses itself upon the attention only when persons at the extremes of age are spoken of. Still more absurd would it be to suppose that Herodotus here meant a combination of aged men. Herodotus's own use of language makes it very clear that ἑταιρηίην τῶν ἡλικιωτέων[2] refers to a company of young men,[3]

---

[1] The gloss of Suid. *s.v.* ἡλικιῶται· συμπράκτορες does not give the classical usage.

[2] Lange's emendation of ἡλικιωτέων to ἐτῶν or συνετῶν (*De Ephet. nom. comm.*, Leipsic, 1873, pp. 22, 23) is wholly unnecessary. Cf. Schömann, *Jahrb. f. Philol.* III (1875), p. 449; also Schöll, quoted *ib.* p. 177.

[3] In the absence of an adequate lexicographical index to Herodotus, the following summary of uses may be helpful (Stein's text) : —

ἡλικιώτης is not elsewhere found in Herod., but its meaning may be inferred from the uses of ἡλικία and its cognates. ἡλικία (1) ʻ time of life,ʼ ʻ age,ʼ *aetas :* τὴν αὐτὴν ἡλικίην (ἔχων, ἔχοντας, ἐχόντων, with dative), III. 16, III. 14; κατ᾽ ἡλικίην τε καὶ φιλότητα, I. 172; νέος ... ἡλικίην, III. 134, VI. 43; of old age, οὖρος δὲ ἡλικίης ... ἄλλος οὐδείς, I. 216; ἐς τόδε ἡλικίης ἥκοντα, VII. 38 : with number of years, ἐὸν ἐτέων ὀκτὼ ἢ ἐννέα ἡλικίην, V. 51; ἡλικίην ... ἐπτακαίδεκα ... γεγονώς, III. 50; ἡλικίην ἐς εἴκοσι ... ἔτεα, I. 209. (2) Of im-

and this is sustained, not only by the striking words ἐκόμησε ἐπὶ τυραννίδι, — when Herodotus speaks of the ambition of the mature Peisistratus he says καταφρονήσας τὴν τυραννίδα (I. 59 ; *cf.* I. 66), — but also by the context : the deed is portrayed — briefly, to be sure,

---

pulses and feelings peculiar or proper to one's years: (of 'youthful' passion), μὴ πάντα ἡλικίη καὶ θυμῷ ἐπίτραπε III. 36 and εἶκε τῇ ἡλικίῃ, VII. 18; (of an old man), V. 19. For III. 36, cf. νεανίας in lexx. (3) 'Time,' Ἡσίοδον ... καὶ Ὅμηρον ἡλικίην τετρακοσίοισι ἔτεσι δοκέω μευ πρεσβυτέρους γενέσθαι, II. 53; 'period,' ταῦτα ἡλικίην εἴη ἂν κατὰ Λάιον, V. 59; Σκαῖος ... ἡλικίην κατ' Οἰδίπουν, V. 60; ταῦτα πρὸ τῆς Πεισιστράτου ἡλικίης ἐγένετο, V. 71; (4) 'proper age for,' οὐ γὰρ εἶχέ πω ἡλικίην στρατεύεσθαι, I. 129. In III. 16, τὴν αὐτὴν ἡλικίην carries also with it the idea of size. As 'age' in English connotes, when used alone, 'old' age, so ἡλικία to the Greeks suggested 'youth,' 'prime.'

Light on the meaning of ἡλικιῶται comes also from the cognates: τῶν ἡλίκων ... πρῶτος, I. 34; τῶν ἡλίκων ἀνδρειοτάτῳ, I. 123; οἱ ὁμήλικες, I. 99. ἡλικιῶται is thus equivalent to οἱ τὴν αὐτὴν ἡλικίην ἔχοντες (Suid. ἡλικιώτης· τῆς αὐτῆς μετεσχηκὼς ἡλικίας). Such persons are united in interests and tastes (ἥλικα γὰρ ὁ παλαιὸς λόγος τέρπειν τὸν ἥλικα, Plat. *Phaedr.* 240 c) as well as in years. That the word does not elsewhere occur in Herodotus should not arouse suspicion; he had several ways of expressing the idea (see examples above). It frequently occurs in Plato (cf. Ast, *Lex. s.v.*), and in the orators in the sense used by Herodotus.

ἑταιρηίην is another ἅπαξ λεγόμενον in Herodotus; its meaning, however, is clear from passages where the concrete word is used : ἑταῖρος, sing. 'comrade,' masc. III. 14 (*bis*), VI. 62 (*ter*); fem. II. 134 (of Rhodope, ἑταίρης γυναικός, *i.e.* 'hetaera'); plu. masc. only III. 125 (ἀγόμενος ... πολλοὺς τῶν ἑταίρων), fem. III. 51, and (of the 'hetaerae' of Naucratis) II. 135. Add τῶν συνεταίρων, VII. 193 (of Jason and his comrades on the Argo); Δία ... ἑταιρήιον, I. 44 (*bis*) and the verb προσεταιρίσασθαι, III. 70 (*bis*) ; προσεταιρίζεται, V. 66 (Cleisthenes and the Athenian δῆμος). If there were more examples preserving the same proportions, one might infer that ἑταιρηίη (or συνέταιροι) was Herodotus's plural for ἑταῖρος. At all events, ἑταιρηίη τῶν ἡλικιωτέων, as used by Herodotus, is the exact equivalent of ἡλικιῶται καὶ ἑταῖροι (Plat. *Symp.* 183 c).

Finally, one might be tempted to suppose that Herod., using the language of the Attic Greeks, when political ἑταιρεῖαι prevailed (Vischer, *Kl. Schriften*, I. pp. 153-204, especially p. 156), intended to describe Cylon's band as a club of a similar sort (cf. Aristot. *Respub. Ath.* c. 20, ἡττωμένος δὲ ταῖς ἑταιρείαις ὁ Κλεισθένης, following Herod. V. 66, but not verbatim). This is possible, but hardly probable. Even if this had been his meaning, he would have been guilty of an anachronism. Solon's σύνοδοι (*Frag.* 4. 22; cf. Plato, *Theaet.* 173 D, σπουδαὶ δὲ ἑταιριῶν ἐπ' ἀρχὰς καὶ σύνοδοι καὶ δεῖπνα κ.τ.λ.), to which appeal might be made, probably does not refer to such combinations as that of Cylon, young revolutionary spirits aided by foreign mercenaries, but rather to the factional

but vividly and with no uncertain lines—as a deed of youthful and heedless daring and violence.

Now we know that Cylon was winner in the δίαυλος at Olympia in 640 B.C. The nature of this contest was such that only men in the flower and vigor of young manhood could participate in it; at this time, then, Cylon must have been still a young man, certainly not above thirty years of age, and probably younger. In twenty or more years after 640 B.C., *i.e.* after 620 B.C., language such as Herodotus uses could not have been applied to him. At the time of his attempt to make himself tyrant of Athens he certainly cannot have been over forty years of age—in all probability he was much younger; hence this episode in his life must have taken place before 621 B.C. (Draco's legislation), and probably much nearer 628 B.C., or even 636 B.C., than 621 B.C.

The only objections that can be offered to this reasoning must be based either on a supposed inaccuracy in the language of Herodotus,

---

combinations of families and their adherents ('Αλκμεωνίδαι καὶ οἱ συστασιῶται, Herod. V. 70) against each other, which were a prominent feature of the times (στάσιν ἔμφυλον, *Frag.* 4. 19; cf. Aristot. *Respub. Ath.* c. 13).

That the language of Herodotus would have been unusual, to say the least, had he intended here to describe the attempt of a political faction led by a man of mature years, must be evident. That this cannot have been his meaning will be clear from a consideration of the several ways in which he speaks of such attempts. The members of parties of this sort are called στασιῶται (the occasion of the formation of στάσεις is that an ambitious man wishes to become κορυφαῖος, III. 82), I. 59, 173; III. 83, 144; V. 36, 72 (of Isagoras and his men), 70 (adherents of Alcmeonidae, under Cleisthenes, reaching back to Cylon's time); VIII. 132. Especially significant is I. 59, καταφρονήσας τὴν τυραννίδα ἤγειρε τρίτην στάσιν, συλλέξας δὲ στασιώτας κ.τ.λ. (of Peisistratus). In I. 96 Deioces, ἀνὴρ ... σοφὸς ... ἐρασθεὶς τυραννίδος ἐποίεε τοίαδε, and in V. 46 Euryleon, τυραννίδι ἐπεχείρησε Σελινοῦντος (καὶ ἐμουνάρχησε χρόνον ἐπ' ὀλίγον; his fate, however, has a suggestive resemblance to that of the Cylonians: οἱ γάρ μιν Σελινούσιοι ἐπαναστάντες ἀπέκτειναν καταφυγόντα ἐπὶ Διὸς ἀγοραίου βωμόν). These passages raise the strong presumption that if Herodotus had meant by the attempt of Cylon an affair like those of Peisistratus, Deioces, or Euryleon, he would have used different language. The meaning of the word ἐκόμησε (ἐπὶ τυραννίδι) as describing the feeling more natural for a youth (Stein, *ap.* Busolt, *G. G.* I. pp. 505, note 2) cannot be pressed; for though the word in this sense is an ἅπαξ λεγόμενον in Herodotus,—it occurs several times in a literal sense: *e.g.* I. 195; II. 36; IV. 168, 180, 191,—it is not much stronger than the word ἐρασθείς used of the sage Deioces's feeling.

or on a supposed untrustworthiness of the date of Cylon's Olympic victory. As to this second point, it may be said that if any matters in Greek chronology rest on a secure basis, the best attested are the dates of Olympic victors, after those records were begun ; and there is no reason, from the records, why this date of Cylon's victory should be regarded with suspicion. Indeed, if the date were a forged date, inserted in the lists without authority, we should have looked for it somewhat later ; Solon was supposed to have been concerned with the efforts to purify the city of the Cylonian sacrilege, and an inventor of this date would have placed it much nearer Solon's time than 640 B.C.

It must be plain to every reader of the passage from Herodotus that there was no uncertainty in the historian's mind as to the nature of the attempt of Cylon, and as to the age of the young adventurers. Where did he gain this impression? The tradition of the affair, in all its essential features, was still definite and clear among the Alcmeonidae when Herodotus visited Athens and heard tales of the house from them or their sympathizers: no story could be more vivid in all its details than that of the youthful, heedless adventurer, ill-prepared, speedily overwhelmed, his company either slain or exiled. Alcmeonidae at least would never have transformed, in their traditions, a powerful enemy, in the maturity of his strength, into a daring, foolish boy. Later on some of these features, the more picturesque as contrasted with the more essential, faded from the historical consciousness.

There is nothing whatever in any of the other authorities that makes our inferences as to Cylon's age improbable. It is true that in none of the accounts is the fact distinctly stated that Cylon was a young man, and it may be claimed that had this been the case, it would have been dwelt upon, especially by Thucydides, whose narrative is very explicit. It is noteworthy, however, that in the earliest of the authorities this aspect of the matter is made clear ; in the subsequent accounts other features of the interesting incident attracted attention and were emphasized.

In his walk upon the acropolis of Athens, Pausanias [1] saw, evidently

---

[1] Paus. I. 28. I. It makes no difference, for our purpose, whether Pausanias saw the statue himself, or merely read about it in his authority. The explicit and

near the great Athena πυλαίμαχος, a statue of Cylon, the presence of which in that place — the statue of a man who had attempted to make himself tyrant — was a mystery to him. The explanation which he suggests, though undoubtedly an incorrect one, carries with it a bit of information that bears upon the matter of the age of Cylon at the time of his attempted usurpation : the statue was of a man εἶδος κάλλιστος. Such language could hardly have been used except of the statue of one in the early prime and beauty of youth. In this statue, then, made doubtless long after the event, probably after the Persian wars[1] and perhaps in the Periclean age, — if not as a substitute for a figure set up very soon after the event[2] and destroyed at

---

somewhat recondite information that he furnishes about Cylon is clearly taken from some book in which matters of interest concerning these ἀναθήματα were given (Polemon, drawing from Atthid-writers, and other sources).

[1] In the Persian occupation of Athens, the Acropolis was cleared of nearly everything. Herod. VIII. 53.

[2] The dedication of the statue here, near the temple of outraged Athena Polias, was intended as a sort of expiation for the guilt of sacrilegious murder. The statue was set up either by the offenders, or by their friends, or by the state, either immediately after the event, which is unlikely, or at some much later time, when it should have seemed that the crime had not been fully expiated. Now since we know that Cylon escaped, this proceeding is more likely to have taken place a long time after the event, when the fact of his escape had become obscured. In answer to the demands of the Lacedaemonians, at the opening of the Peloponnesian war, that Pericles should be cast out, as tainted by ancient sacrilege, — τοῦτο τὸ ἄγος ἐλαύνειν, — the Athenians made the counter-demand that the Spartans should free themselves of the taint of the crime committed against Athena Chalcioecus, *i.e.* the starving of King Pausanias in the temple of Athena at Sparta, thirty (Ad. Bauer, *l.c.* pp. 70, 72) years or more earlier. The Spartans had, however, in compliance with the direction of the god of Delphi, already offered "two bodies for the one," two bronze statues of Pausanias, which were set up near the temple (Thuc. I. 127, 128, 134, 135; cf. also Paus. III. 17. 7-9). From this language one might perhaps infer that the Athenians had already done their utmost in atonement for the Cylonian sacrilege : had, among other things, already dedicated on the Acropolis a statue of Cylon.

The existence of this statue of Cylon can hardly be explained in connexion with the curious regulation with reference to the archons, whereby on entering office they solemnly swore that, if they should transgress any of the laws, they would dedicate a golden statue (οἱ δὲ ἐννέα ἄρχοντες ὀμνύντες πρὸς τῷ λίθῳ κατεφάτιζον ἀναθήσειν ἀνδριάντα χρυσοῦν ἐάν τινα παραβῶσι τῶν νόμων, Aristot. *Respub. Ath.* c. 7; cf. Heracl. *Exc. Pol.* 8; Pollux VIII. 86; Suid. *s.v.* χρυσῆ εἰκών). In Plato (*Phaedr.* 235 E) Socrates playfully embroiders this oath, and adds unessential details

ihe time of the Persian occupation of the acropolis, perhaps as a sort of an expiatory offering made by the friends of Pericles at the time when party strife had made his hereditary taint as an Alcmeonid a factor of great weight against him,[1] — we have a survival of the authentic tradition, elsewhere meeting us only in Herodotus, that Cylon was a young man at the time of his attempt.

A second class of arguments in favor of a date for Cylon earlier than 621 B.C. may be based upon the probable age of the Megacles prominent in the affair as the archon who broke his word, and, at the head of a faction, committed sacrilegious murder. The age of this man at this time is to be inferred from that of his son Alcmeon, general of the Athenians in the First Sacred War. A discussion of this topic raises several related questions concerning the chronology, fortunes, and wealth of the Alcmeonidae in the latter part of the seventh and in the first half of the sixth centuries B.C.

## VI.

### THE ALCMEONIDAE BEFORE PEISISTRATUS.

According to Attic traditions the noble house of the Alcmeonidae[2] had in the earliest historic period shown its pre-eminence : two of its members, Megacles and Alcmeon, had been so-called life-archons, the later being the last in that series.[3] Uncertain as this tra-

---

($\chi\rho\nu\sigma\tilde{\eta}\nu$ $\epsilon\dot{\iota}\kappa\delta\nu\alpha$ $\dot{\iota}\sigma\sigma\mu\acute{\epsilon}\tau\rho\eta\tau\sigma\nu$ $\epsilon\dot{\iota}s$ $\Delta\epsilon\lambda\phi\sigma\dot{\nu}s$ $\dot{\alpha}\nu\alpha\theta\acute{\eta}\sigma\epsilon\iota\nu$, but Plutarch (*Sol.* 25), not seeing the fun, reproduces the whole passage from Plato as the ancient regulation). The statuette here provided for was of gold, and was evidently intended as a penalty for receiving bribes in office, not for other forms of malfeasance, and doubtless would have been a statuette of some divinity, probably Athena, whose treasure had been appropriated. The statue of Cylon, however, mentioned by Pausanias, was a portrait statue of bronze. Pre-Solonian archons could hardly have dedicated such a statue. Furthermore, pre-Solonian archons would have known that Cylon had escaped.

[1] This statue seems to have stood not far from one of Pericles: Paus. I. 25. 1 and 28. 1.

[2] Alcmeon (Alcmeonidae), not Alcmaeon, is the spelling of the Attic inscriptions, *e.g.* C.I.A., IV[b] 373, n. 189, p. 98 (sixth century B.C.). Cf. Meisterhans, *Gramm.*[2] § 14, p. 28, and notes 167 and 517. Euripides's play was entitled Ἀλκμέων, Cramer, *Anec. Oxon.* II. p. 337. 4. Ἀλκμεωνίδαι, Dem. XXI. 144 (Σ).

[3] In the list (Euseb. *Chron.* I. 185 ff.) of thirteen life-archons, beginning with

dition may be, there is no uncertainty about the tradition that makes this family one of the noble γένη, later called Eupatridae,[1] — from

Medon, the sixth is Megacles and the thirteenth Alcmeon. The periods ascribed to these archons, who lived before ἀναγραφαί were begun, are purely conjectural. The presence of these names in this list, as also of the names of Agamestor (Philaïd?), and Ariphron (Buzygid), and others, shows one of three things: either (1) that the tradition that the succession was limited to Medontidae, and so continued into the period of the decennial archontate (Paus. I. 3. 3; IV. 5. 10; 13. 7), was false; or (2) that these men were Medontidae on their mothers' side, but on their fathers' side members of other families; or (3) that these names do not belong in the historic series, the ancient list having been revised by the insertion, at a late period, of well-known Attic names. Cf. Busolt, *G. G.* I. p. 406, note 2.

[1] The answer to the question as to whether the Alcmeonidae were Eupatridae (denied by Sauppe, Stein — on Herod. I. 59 — and others; affirmed by Vischer and others) will depend upon the sense in which we are to take the word: whether (1) as the name of an Attic γένος, Εὐπατρίδαι, or (2) εὐπατρίδαι, as the generic name of a political class, an estate (Germ. 'Stand'), composed of certain ancient noble-born families, possessing certain traditional political rights and privileges. That there was such an Attic γένος is clear: see Isocr. XVI. 25, Dem. XXI. 144; Polemon, *ap.* Schol. Soph. *O. C.* 489 (cf. Wilamowitz, *Phil. Unt.* I. 119, note, and *Hermes*, 22 [1887], pp. 121, and 479 ff. [Töpffer]; also Hirzel, *Rhein. Mus.* [1888], p. 631, but especially Töpffer, *Att. Gen.* pp. 175 ff.); that the Alcmeonidae did not belong to it is equally clear (cf. Isocr. *l.c.*). That, however, the Alcmeonidae were an ancient family, and that its members enjoyed the highest privileges, in the state, of holding office, etc., is also demonstrable (cf. Vischer, *Kl. Schriften*, I. pp. 401 ff.). The scolion preserved in Aristot. *Respub. Ath.* c. 19, and often quoted (see Rose, *Aristot. Fragm.* 394, and *Aristot. Pseudepigr.* pp. 417, 418), shows that in the mouths of the people the Alcmeonidae were early called εὐπατρίδαι, whatever the word may have meant: αἰαῖ Λειψύδριον προδωσέταιρον | οἵους ἄνδρας ἀπώλεσας μάχεσθαι | ἀγαθούς τε καὶ εὐπατρίδας | οἳ τότ' ἔδειξαν οἵων | πατέρων ἔσαν.

From the extreme rarity, if not entire absence, of the word εὐπατρίδαι in prose-writers before Aristotle, to designate a political office-holding class of nobles as contrasted with the low-born populace (*i.e.* in the sense of Lat. *optimates, patricii*), — perhaps because the word had already been taken up in the name of the γένος Εὐπατρίδαι (cf. Isocr. XVI. 25), — and from the use, where we should look for it, of οἱ εὐγενεῖς, τὰ γένη, οἱ δυνατοί, οἱ λαμπροί, οἱ ἐκ τῶν γένων, οἱ γνώριμοι, etc., one might raise the question whether εὐπατρίδαι, at least before the time of Aristotle, was naturally and generally understood in this special sense. A poetical word originally (Soph. *El.* 160, 857, Eur. *Alc.* 920), it had more than one meaning: 'good or true to one's father' — so of Orestes, perhaps the reputed founder of the γένος Εὐπατρίδαι (Hirzel, *Rhein. Mus.* 43 [1888], p. 631) — or 'of good parent-

which archons were chosen, — and that connects its members with many important phases of Attic history from the latter half of the seventh century B.C. onward. The Alcmeonidae first meet us in connexion with the affair of Cylon, and their attitude in this matter raises a question as to the causes of their activity. Did they assail and suppress Cylon only as the head or representative of a rival family, wishing to retain for themselves the pre-eminence which the election of one or more of their number to the archonship bears witness to? Or did they act rather as patriots, defenders of the state against tyrants, — μισοτύραννοι, as Herodotus calls them — with disinterested motives? Or were they merely public officers doing their official duty in quelling a sedition and uprising that threatened the existence of the state? The violence with which they acted, disregarding the holiest laws which made the suppliant sacred, shows that this last explanation is inadequate. A definitive answer can hardly be given: doubtless several or even all of these considerations combined as motives. Aristotle's διὰ τὴν πρὸς ἀλλήλους φιλονικίαν, said of the party strug-

---

age.' It may have been adopted by Aristotle in a technical sense, — in part because of one of its meanings; in part perhaps because of the representative character of the family Εὐπατρίδαι, just as in Roman times Eteobutadae was used as the synonyme of εὐγενεῖs (Töpffer, *Att. Geneal.* p. 117), — and later on, especially in Roman times, when the analogy of Roman political conditions affected the scholar's conceptions, it may have become thoroughly established in this sense. Thus Plut. uses it for the Latin patricians (*Fab.* 16, *Popl.* 18); and in Dion. Hal. *Ant.* II. 8, εὐπατρίδαι is Greek for *patricii*, as ἄγροικοι for *plebeii*. Landwehr, *Philol.* Suppl.-Bd. V. (1884) pp. 143 ff., has the examples; cf. also Busolt, *G. G.* I. pp. 387–89, for the bibliography.

It should be added that Aristotle himself never uses the word in the *Politics*, and only twice in *Respub. Ath.* (cc. 13, 19), elsewhere preferring, where this would seem to have been the natural expression, other words (οἱ γνώριμοι, etc.). It is doubtful — a third possible case — whether this word was found in Aristotle's account of the Attic state under Theseus, in the lost part of the *Respub. Ath.* (Rose, *Aristot. Fragm.* 384, 385). It is not given (as Kenyon remarks, p. 173) in the early versions of this passage (*Lex. Dem. Patm.* p. 152 — Sakkelion, *Bull. Corr. Hellén.* I. 1877; — Schol. Plat. *Axioch.* 371 D; Moeris, *Lex. Att.* p. 193), though it occurs in the paraphrase in Plut. *Thes.* 25, and in Pollux VIII. 111. The last version is in part, at least, demonstrably an expansion, by the insertion of the words ἐξ εὐπατριδῶν, of the language of Aristotle (*Respub. Ath.* c. 8: φυλαὶ δ᾽ ἦσαν δ᾽ καθάπερ πρότερον καὶ φυλοβασιλεῖς τέτταρες, κ.τ.λ. Pollux., *ib.*: οἱ δὲ φυλοβασιλεῖς ἐξ εὐπατριδῶν δ᾽ ὄντες, κ.τ.λ.).

gles immediately after Solon's reforms, points, as we have already remarked, to early family rivalries. Friends of the Alcmeonidae in subsequent centuries, as they looked back upon the history of the family, in which prominent members stand forth as the enemies of tyrants and as the upholders of the people against oligarchical domination, saw in this house ideal champions of the liberty of the people, but they viewed history with false perspective.[1] Megacles, the younger, who, at the head of the Parali, withstood Peisistratus, champion of the Diacrii, did so, — as also Lycurgus, the leader of the Pediaei, — not with high motives, but because he hoped to gain something by it, and in particular a mastery over his rivals. The subsequent compromise proposed by Megacles to Peisistratus, whereby the tyrant having married his daughter should receive Megacles's support in his usurpation, is hardly the conduct of a pure-minded patriot.[2] When finally the Peisistratidae were cast out, in large measure through the efforts of the outraged Alcmeonidae, and Cleisthenes, the son of Megacles, with his adherents gained the ascendancy in the state, as over-against his oligarchic rivals now headed by Isagoras, it was apparently mainly to establish himself and his party in power that he instituted his far-reaching reforms.[3]   At

---

[1] Cf. especially Isocr. XVI. 25, who celebrates the wealth and patriotic spirit of the family : οἱ τοῦ μὲν πλούτου μέγιστον μνημεῖον κατέλιπον — ἵππων γὰρ ζεύγει πρῶτος Ἀλκμέων τῶν πολιτῶν Ὀλυμπίασιν ἐνίκησε — τὴν δ᾽ εὔνοιαν ἣν εἶχον εἰς τὸ πλῆθος ἐν τοῖς τυραννικοῖς ἐπεδείξαντο ... οὐκ ἠξίωσαν μετασχεῖν τῆς ἐκείνου (*i.e.* Peisistratus) τυραννίδος ἀλλ᾽ εἵλοντο φυγεῖν μᾶλλον ἢ τοὺς πολίτας ἰδεῖν δουλεύοντας, κ.τ.λ. Modern instances of a similar lack of historical perspective abound.

[2] Plut. *Sol.* 29 : πράγματα νεώτερα προσδοκᾶν καὶ ποθεῖν ἅπαντας (*i.e.* these party leaders) ἑτέραν κατάστασιν, οὐκ ἴσον ἐλπίζοντας, ἀλλὰ πλέον ἕξειν ἐν τῇ μεταβολῇ καὶ κρατήσειν παντάπασι τῶν διαφερομένων. Herod. I. 59, 60 : ἔνθα δὴ ὁ Πεισίστρατος ἦρχε Ἀθηναίων. The factions of Lycurgus and Megacles combine against Peisistratus and cast him out; they subsequently fall out among themselves, and Megacles makes a compromise with Peisistratus, offering his daughter in marriage (ἐπὶ τυραννίδι).

[3] Herod. V. 66 : οὗτοι οἱ ἄνδρες ἐστασίασαν περὶ δυνάμιος, ἐσσούμενος δὲ ὁ Κλεισθένης τὸν δῆμον προσεταιρίζεται, as more than a century earlier, for a practically similar purpose, Cylon had called to his aid an ἑταιρήιην τῶν ἡλικιωτέων. Aristotle's language is (*Respub. Ath.* c. 20) : ἐστασίαζον πρὸς ἀλλήλους Ἰσαγόρας ... καὶ Κλεισθένης ... ἡττώμενος δὲ ταῖς ἑταιρείαις ὁ Κλεισθένης προσηγάγετο τὸν δῆμον, ἀποδιδοὺς τῷ πλήθει τὴν πολιτείαν (see above, p. 38, note). The radical

no point in the political history of the family — except, perhaps, in some of the acts of its greatest scion, Pericles — do we find evidence of wholly disinterested and patriotic conduct; misfortune, exile, and many other reverses, together with signal success in the gaining of wealth, uniting its members closely, had strongly developed the family feeling, and had taught them insight and political wisdom, which, when the opportunity arrived, they put to brilliant use to their own great advantage, as also to that of the state.

According to the clear language of Thucydides the attempt of Cylon was brought to a summary end by an uprising of the people, hastening in from the country, followed by violent measures on the part of the Alcmeonidae. The interests of the Alcmeonidae are here served by the people from the country: the family may be regarded as now standing at the head of the second of the two great classes into which from early times the Athenian people fall, — the class whom Aristotle calls ἄποικοι, and which would at this time include the artisan as well as the peasant class. Though the lines appear sharply drawn between the well-to-do and the poor, there is as yet no evidence of minuter subdivisions according to class differences, nor according to local factions, which meet us in quick succession soon after Solon's legislation. Two generations later the family appears — in the person of Megacles, grandson of the Megacles of the affair of Cylon — as the champion of the local faction of the Parali, social and economic changes having come about that led most naturally to this relation; three generations later it is the people (*Demus*) as such that Cleisthenes allies to himself; five generations later it is by his extraordinary services to the Demus that Pericles maintains himself in his supreme position; while in the sixth generation the coquettings of

---

character of the reforms of Cleisthenes was doubtless suggested to him by the experience of his grandfather, for whose reorganization of the Sicyon constitution one would hardly claim a patriot's disinterestedness. The ostracism of Megacles, son of Hippocrates and nephew of Cleisthenes, in 487/6 B.C., as supporter of the Peisistratidae shows that the family had no ingrained aversion to tyranny (Aristot. *Respub. Ath.* c. 22). Lysias (XIV. 39; cf. [Andoc.] *Contra Alc.* 34) makes him Cleisthenes's son, grandfather of Alcibiades, — hence perhaps the δίς. See also the ostrakon bearing the name of Megacles, son of Hippocrates, the person mentioned by Aristotle (Benndorf, *Griech. u. Sicil. Vasenbilder*, p. 50, pl. 29, no. 10); and a pinax discussed by Studniczka (*Jahrb. d. Arch. Inst.* 2. [1887], p. 161).

the Alcmeonid Alcibiades with the same Demus are the causes at once of his rise and of his fall.

The affair of Cylon, marked as it was by violence and unholy bloodshed, was followed by a long period of strife. The survivors of the Cylonians and their adherents gain strength, and a reaction against the Alcmeonidae sets in, mainly political,[1] but doubtless sharpened by the superstitious sense of outraged divine law. The people are at variance and in dread of worse ill; according to some authorities Solon,[2] then beginning to rise into prominence, having the confidence of both parties, or some other influential citizen, prevails upon the Alcmeonidae to submit to the verdict of trial by a special court of three hundred citizens selected for this purpose. The formal accuser, as we have seen, is Myron, a Lycomid; the Alcmeonidae are found guilty; the bodies of the dead offenders are dug up and cast beyond the borders; the living relatives withdraw, condemned to perpetual exile.[3]

The trial and exile of the Alcmeonidae must have taken place no little time before the legislation of Solon, and before the breaking out of the Sacred War, in which Alcmeon, now head of the house, is general of the Athenian contingent.[4] There are two grounds for

---

[1] Cf. Schömann, *Jahrb. f. Philol.* 111 (:875), pp. 464 ff.

[2] The connexion of Solon with this trial has only slight evidence to sustain it. Niese, *Zur Gesch. Solons*, p. 14.

[3] Unless the detail about the ἐξορισμός of the bodies of the dead be a dittography for what was said of the procedure in the time of Cleisthenes (an unlikely hypothesis; see above, p. 17, note 1), one must infer that a considerable time had elapsed between the sacrilege and the trial. Aristotle's language suggests that Megacles, the chief culprit, was one of the dead; at all events, we hear nothing of him again. Diels (*Sitzungsb. d. Berl. Akad.*, 1891, p. 388) supposes a generation to have passed.

[4] The main ground for a later date of the trial is the supposed connexion of Epimenides with the measures taken for the purification of the city from the Κυλώνειον ἄγος. According to this view, the trial must have taken place, if not after the arrival of Epimenides, — according to one account (Diog. Laert. I. 10. 110; cf. Suid. *s.v.* 'Επιμενίδης for another date) he came Ol. 42. 1 = 596 B.C., — at least shortly before it. Thus Schömann — who fixes the date of the affair of Cylon at 612 B.C., and not, as we would, a dozen or more years earlier — would put the trial after the beginning of the Sacred War (by him dated 600 B.C.), and before Epimenides (596 B.C.): after the beginning of the war, because otherwise Alcmeon could hardly have been chosen general; before Epimenides, because in

this inference : first, the selection of Alcmeon as representative of the Athenian people in the war for the honor of Delphi, and, secondly, the fact that a reaction had set in against the Cylonians before the enactment of Solon's laws. Both of these things would have been impossible but for a considerable lapse of time. We must conceive of the case somewhat as follows : after the departure of the Alcmeonidae, the keenness of the feeling of hatred (ἐναγεῖς ἐμισοῦντο) which prompted the severity of their punishment became less and less sharp, — in part because of the natural reaction that sets in in all such cases ; in part doubtless because of the good report that came home of the brave and wise conduct of the members of the family in their absence, and especially of Alcmeon ; in part also because of new ties of business formed between enterprising Athenians at home and the absent Alcmeonidae, who were now in all probability adventuring themselves in trade and commerce in foreign lands, and thus laying the foundations of the wealth for which in subsequent times their family was illustrious. With the growth and spread of this feeling in favor of the Alcmeonidae — the most conspicuous evidence of which was the choice of Alcmeon as general, and the restoration of the family therein involved — there went also a deepening of the feeling against the Cylonians, which is clearly expressed in the language of the amnesty-law of Solon, given in the thirteenth ἄξων.[1]

---

the accounts of the activity of Epimenides in purifying the city, no mention is made of the trial and exile. But — to leave out of consideration the very questionable date of the Sacred War assumed by Schömann and the fact that the order of events in Aristotle's narrative (*Respub. Ath.* cc. 1 ff.) points conclusively to a trial of the Alcmeonidae, if not before Draco, certainly not long after him, — it is highly improbable that Solon's amnesty-law (Plut. *Sol.* 19) should have allowed the return of the exiles only a few months after their awful banishment, while making an express exception in the case of the exiled Cylonians. Further, as will be shown later (pp. 69 ff.), the connexion of Epimenides with this affair, at least as late as 596 B.C., is problematical, and arguments based upon it have little weight.

[1] Plut. *Sol.* 19 : this law, which provides for pardon and restoration to rights of citizenship, makes exception in the case of the Cylonians, in the words πλὴν ὅσοι . . . ἐκ πρυτανείου καταδικασθέντες . . . ἐπὶ τυραννίδι ἔφευγον. Even if, with Lipsius-Schömann (*Att. Proc.* I. p. 27), we deny that the court before which the Cylonians were tried was an archon's court, there can be no doubt that in these words the Cylonians are meant. The εἰς τὴν κρίσιν . . . ἐν Ἀρείῳ πάγῳ of Schol. I. Ar. *Eq.* 445 is a mistaken form of statement, which has no weight. See pp. 16, 24, and note 1.

All such changes of popular feeling take time, and we can hardly be wrong in insisting that between the affair of Cylon, which was the original cause of all these changes of mental attitude, and the later exhibitions of popular feeling in the matter, a period of many years must have elapsed.

In the generation in which the attempt of Cylon was thwarted, the conspicuous Alcmeonid is Megacles. In the next generation the leading member of the family is Alcmeon, the son of Megacles, noted for the part he took in the Sacred War and for his great wealth.[1] About the exact date and length of the Sacred War there is still ground for uncertainty, though there is every probability that the war practically closed in the archonship at Athens of Simon (*i.e.* 590 B.C.) ;[2] its duration is wholly uncertain, since we must regard the ten-year period ascribed to it by later writers[3] as a sort of anachronistic echo of the ten-year period of the Sacred War in the fourth century B.C. (357–346 B.C.), if not suggested by the legend of the Trojan War. This first Sacred War, though not so great an affair as it was made out to be in much later times,[4] still has something of a universal character, the several tribes of the Delphian amphictyony taking sides : the leader of the Athenian contingent in it, — according to the best records, the Delphic ὑπομνήματα — was Alcmeon.[5] It is reasonable

---

[1] Plut. *Sol.* 11; Herod. VI. 125; Isocr. XVI. 25.

[2] Simon, archon Ol. 47. 3; Mar. Par. Ep. 37. For a discussion of the date of the founding of the Pythian στεφανίτης ἀγών, which is connected with that of the Sacred War, see Landwehr, *Philol.* Suppl.-Bd. V. (1884), pp. 105-114. Ad. Bauer, *l.c.* p. 48, discussing the subject in the light of the recovered *Respub. Ath.*, sets this date at B.C. 583; Damasias he would place B.C. 583-1, understanding the δευτέρου of Mar. Par. Ep. 38 to refer not to Damasias's second year, but to Damasias II. (Damasias I., archon in B.C. 639/8; Dion. Hal. *Ant.* III. 38).

[3] Callisthenes, *ap.* Athen. XIII. 560 C. Cf. Niese, *Zur Gesch. Solons*, pp. 16 ff.

[4] Thuc. I. 15.

[5] Plut. *Sol.* 11 : ἔν τε τοῖς Δελφῶν ὑπομνήμασιν Ἀλκμαίων . . . Ἀθηναίων στρατηγὸς ἀναγέγραπται. The tradition (Aristot. *Pythion.* and Euanthes the Samian, as quoted by Hermippus, — given us in Plut. *Sol.* 11; also Aesch. *Ctes.* 108) represented Solon as prominent in the agitation that led to the war, and, according to Euanthes, made him general. Even though with Niese (*Zur Gesch. Solons*, p. 17) we may be disposed to look upon this as a pleasing Aeschinean fiction (Dem. *Cor.* 149, λόγους εὐπροσώπους καὶ μύθους ὅθεν ἡ Κιρραία χώρα καθιερώθη συνθεὶς καὶ διεξελθών), a proceeding which the quotation from Aristotle (πεισθέντες γὰρ ὑπ' ἐκείνου πρὸς τὸν πόλεμον ὥρμησαν οἱ Ἀμφικτύονες ὡς ἄλλοι τε μαρτυροῦσι καὶ

to believe that, under all the circumstances, Alcmeon at this time, *i.e.* before 590 B.C., could not have been a young man.[1] The necessary qualifications for the office of general were age, experience, reputation, and these conditions must have been especially required in a candidate belonging to a family upon which the taint still rested. The bearing of this inference upon the main question under discussion will be more evident later on.

The wealth of Alcmeon and its source is a subject deserving examination, especially as the testimonies relating to it are somewhat confused. Herodotus (VI. 125) names Alcmeon as the friend of Croesus, — which is of course impossible, — and gives the well-known story of the origin of his wealth from the gifts of Croesus, and remarks that it was by reason of this wealth that he presented himself at Olympia with a four-horse chariot and won the race ; he also adds that the house was further enriched in the next generation by Cleisthenes of Sicyon, into whose family Megacles, Alcmeon's son, had married. Evidently the same victor and the same victory in the four-horse chariot-race, adduced as an evidence of the wealth of the Alcmeonidae, are celebrated by Isocrates (XVI. 25) ; this victory is by him said to have been the first one of its kind won by an Athenian.[2] Pindar[3] (*Pyth.* 7. 14) declares that one Olympic, five

---

'Αριστοτέλης ἐν τῇ τῶν Πυθιονικῶν ἀναγραφῇ Σόλωνι τὴν γνώμην ἀνατιθείς) ought to make us slow to do, we still have no reason to doubt the part taken in the war by Alcmeon.

[1] Aristot. (*Respub. Ath.* c. 4) asserts that, under the Draconian constitution, which prevailed at the time when Alcmeon was chosen to office, it was required that the generals should be men with a property qualification of not less than one hundred minae, and should have children born in wedlock over ten years of age.

Phrynon, general before Sigeum, about B.C. 610, must have been, at the time of his στρατηγία, not less than forty-five years of age. He won an Olympic victory, Ol. 36 (B.C. 636): in the παγκράτιον, according to Diog. Laert. I. 4. 74; in the stadium (apparently), according to Euseb. I. 199; he fell before Sigeum in a single combat with Pittacus. Probably Jul. Afric. wrote 'Αρυτάμας Λάκων στάδιον. Παγκρατίου Φρύνων 'Αθηναῖος, ὃς Πιττακῷ μονομαχῶν ἀνῃρέθη (Rutgers, *Jul. Afr.* pp. 13, 14; for Artytamas, cf. Antigon. Carystius, *Hist. Mirab.* 121, in Westermann's *Paradoxographi*, p. 90).

[2] The ἵππων τελείων δρόμος . . . was established Ol. 25 (B.C. 680), and the first victor was the Theban Pagondas (Paus. V. S. 7).

[3] Pind. *Pyth.* 7. 13 ff.: ἄγοντι δέ με πέντε μὲν 'Ισθμοῖ | νῖκαι, μία δ' ἐκπρεπὴς | Διὸς 'Ολυμπιάς | δύο δ' ἀπὸ Κίρρας. The contradiction of this statement found in

Isthmian, and two Pythian victories were obtained by members of the family (before B.C. 490). The Scholiast on this passage, though he gives us an extraordinary wreck of details, yet preserves the good tradition (ἀναγράφεται), that this victory was won in Ol. 47 (B.C. 592).[1]

It was traditionally believed, then, that at this early date — about 590 B.C. — the Alcmeonidae were a wealthy family, and the explanation for this wealth was found, perversely and impossibly enough, in a supposed connexion with Croesus. Croesus, however, belonged to the next generation, not ascending the throne before 560 B.C.,[2] though he may have had a share in the government with his father Alyattes

---

Arg. II. Ar. *Nub.* and in Schol. Ar. *Nub.* 64 (Tzetz. *Chil.* I. 8 only follows this Schol.) is sufficiently met by Boeckh, *Pind.* II. 2, pp. 303, 304. The large number of Isthmian victories accredited to the family is doubtless to be explained by the proximity of Sicyon to the place of the games: Sicyon must have been to Megacles, the husband of Agariste, and to their immediate descendants, a second home. According to Krause's lists (*Pythien, Nem. u. Isth.* pp. 209–23), the cities that furnished much the larger number of Isthmian victors were Corinth, Aegina, and Sicyon; Athens is only slightly represented. This shows that there were exceptional reasons — probably due to local causes — why the Alcmeonidae were often at these games.

[1] Boeckh, *Pind.* II. 1, p. 391. In the Schol. the name of the victor is wrongly given as Megacles, a reading which Boeckh at first accepted, and accordingly identifying this Megacles with the Cylonian Megacles, he brought down the date of Cylon to suit (B.C. 599). In the commentary on the passage Boeckh withdraws this identification (II. 2, p. 304: "meam ad Scholia olim proditam opinionem removero"), and would emend the date to Ol. 57, — without, however, withdrawing the date for Cylon, — and refer the victory to Megacles, the contemporary of Peisistratus (Schol. Ar. *Nub.* 64). This latter victory, by the way, is, on the face of it, wrongly ascribed to Megacles; the Schol. has confused the name of Megacles with that of Cimon (Herod. VI. 35, 36; VI. 103), and ascribes to the former what belongs to the latter (cf. Krause, *Olympia*, p. 324). The confusion of names in the Schol. is not surprising; as the orators confuse the names of Miltiades and Cimon, as Herodotus, Aelian, and Paus. (VI. 19. 6) furnish similar instances, it is to be expected that a less familiar Alcmeon should be turned into a more familiar Megacles. Cf. Töpffer, *Att. Gen.* p. 280, note.

[2] Croesus's reign probably ceased 546 B.C.: he marched against Cyrus B.C. 548, Ol. 58. 1 (Euseb. I. 96), and was soon defeated, and Sardis was taken (cf. Sosicrates *ap.* Diog. Laert. II. 7. 95): cf. Clinton, *F. H.* II. *s.a.* 546 B.C.: the date of the fall of Sardis was an accepted and well-known epoch (Diels, *Rhein. Mus.* 31, p. 20). Croesus was thirty-five years of age at the death of his father (Herod. I. 26), and reigned fourteen years (Herod. I. 86); the date of his accession to the throne would then be about 560 B.C. For variant dates, see Busolt, *G.G.* I. pp. 332 ff.

for a while before this time. In the light of the statement in Herodotus (I. 19) that Alyattes, having fallen sick, consulted the oracle at Delphi, and of the subsequent statement (VI. 125) that the Lydian king — here, to be sure, named Croesus — in gratitude to Alcmeon for aid rendered his ambassadors invited him to Sardis and vastly enriched him, Schömann[1] makes the ingenious suggestion that Alyattes, not Croesus, was the actual source of the wealth of the Alcmeonidae. The confusion[2] of the son with his father was very natural, especially after Croesus had become the type of the wealthy monarch.[3]

---

[1] Schömann (*Jahrb. f. Philol.* III [1875], p. 466) gives two reasons for believing that Herodotus is wrong in here naming Croesus: Croesus did not ascend the throne until fully thirty years after Alcmeon's στρατηγία, and, secondly, he always stood in too good repute in Delphi to make it likely that his ambassadors needed the aid and special pleadings of others.

[2] Though there are several fictitious features in this story, it is more reasonable to believe that Herodotus has erred in his chronology than that there is no basis of fact whatever for friendly aid given the Alcmeonidae by a Lydian king.

[3] Of course the story in Herodotus (I. 30–33), followed by Plutarch (*Sol.* 27 ff.), which brings Solon and Croesus together, is equally improbable. Plutarch admits the chronological difficulties, but naïvely waives them in the characteristic passage: τὴν πρὸς Κροῖσον ἔντευξιν αὐτοῦ δοκοῦσιν ἔνιοι τοῖς χρόνοις ὡς πεπλασμένην ἐλέγχειν. ἐγὼ δὲ λόγον ἔνδοξον οὕτω ... καὶ, ὃ μεῖζόν ἐστι, πρέποντα τῷ Σόλωνος ἤθει ... οὔ μοι δοκῶ προήσεσθαι χρονικοῖς τισι λεγομένοις κανόσι κ.τ.λ. (*Sol.* 27, *ad init.*). Niese, *Zur Gesch. Solons*, p. 10.

Five instances of error on the part of Herodotus in establishing synchronisms will strike every reader: viz. (1) Herod. I. 29, which brings Solon and Croesus together; (2) Herod. VI. 125, Alcmeon and Croesus; (3) Herod. II. 177, Solon and Amasis; (4) Herod. V. 127, Pheidon of Argos and Megacles, the suitor of Agariste; and (5) Herod. V. 94, 95, where the (original) conquest of Sigeum is ascribed to Peisistratus. Now we must suppose that Herodotus was well informed as regards the chronological position, measured by generations, in relation to himself, of prominent persons living as far back as the middle of the sixth century B.C., *i.e.* one hundred years before his own time (Croesus, Megacles, and perhaps Amasis). It is to be noted that, in all these instances of error, he has merely drawn down into the times known to him personalities belonging to a vaguer, earlier generation: Alcmeon was rich, — hence he must have been the friend of the wealthy Croesus. Solon was a sage, — hence he must have been the adviser of the ill-starred Croesus; also a law-giver, — hence he must have had some connexion with the prince of the land of wise and hoary institutions. Almost everything that Herodotus tells about the intercourse of these persons is of the most general character, like the anecdotes, of a painful family likeness, that are popularly told of all noteworthy personages. With, perhaps, the single excep-

However this may be, there must have been some ground for the tradition that made the Alcmeonidae gain their wealth over seas. I would offer a suggestion as to the source of the ancient wealth of the Alcmeonidae at the time, which, though not certain, seems to have a large degree of probability in it. It is that the Alcmeonidae were among the first foreign traders from Athens, at a time when foreign trade was, for Athens at least, in its inception; that the sure foundations of their activity as traders were laid in their exile, though this activity may have begun yet earlier; that this activity was kept up with such vigor and success after their return, that the head of the house in the generation next following Alcmeon — *i.e.* Megacles the younger — naturally became the leader and representative of the merchant or trading class in the Athenian state. The main argument on which this theory is based is the fact that Megacles was the leader of the Parali. This leadership could not have been due to the accident of local habitation, as Peisistratus's leadership of the Diacrii was perhaps due to the fact that his family home and stronghold was

---

tion of what is related of Solon's debt to Amasis, nothing in these instances has the stamp of a vivid, unique historical reality. The explicit, and apparently more historic, character of the statements in II. 177, to the effect that Solon owed to Amasis what was afterward called the νόμος ἀργίας, gives them the air of greater credibility, and T. Case ( *Class. Review*, 1888, p. 241) does well to call attention to them. On the other hand, however, the tradition as to the origin of this νόμος ἀργίας is so variant in antiquity that we can by no means be certain that Herodotus's form of it is the correct one; thus (1) Lysias, *Contra Nicid.* (*ap.* Diog. Laert. I. 2. 55) asserts that Draco proposed the law, and Draco's connexion with the law further appears from Plut. *Sol.* 17, Phot. *Lex. App.* p. 665, Pollux VIII. 42. (2) Theophrastus asserts that Peisistratus was the author of the law (Plut. *Sol.* 31), while (3) Herodotus (II. 177) ascribes it to Amasis. Now Peisistratus and Amasis were contemporaries; Amasis therefore might be supposed to have suggested the measure to Peisistratus, Amasis being the personal form for Egypt. Herodotus, however, makes Solon the promulgator of all good laws; hence it must have been to Solon that Amasis suggested it. A more probable explanation would deny any personal connexion between Solon and Amasis as the origin of the usage; in ancient times there was both at Athens and in Egypt a law prohibiting idleness; Amasis was the Solon of Egypt, and Solon the Amasis of Greece; Egypt was more ancient than Greece, hence Amasis gave Solon the law. Still again: Solon visited Egypt; what more natural — as Plutarch would say, it is a λόγος πρέπων τῷ Σόλωνος ἤθει — than that the Athenian legislator should have met the Egyptian legislator, and adopted from him the measure which prevailed in both lands?

in the thickly populated Brauronian fastnesses in the upland country of Diacria[1]; the ancient seat of the Alcmeonidae seems to have been, not on the shore, but well up in the Athenian plain, on the slopes of Parnes near Leipsydrium,[2] where many years later they bravely though unsuccessfully withstood the sons of Peisistratus. This leadership can be most intelligibly explained only on the supposition of

---

[1] Plut. *Sol.* 10; Schol. Ar. *Av.* 873; Schol. Ar. *Pac.* 874.

[2] Aristot. *Respub. Ath.* c. 19: Ἀλκμεωνίδαι . . . τειχίσαντες ἐν τῇ χώρᾳ Λειψύδριον τὸ ὑπὲρ [ὑπὸ?] Πάρνηθος, εἰς ὃ συνῆλθόν τινες τῶν ἐκ τοῦ ἄστεως. The text is probably corrupt, since the readings derived from the original text are various, viz. (1) ὑπὲρ Πάρνηθος, Hesych. *s.v.* Λειψύδριον. (2) τὸ ὑπὲρ Πάρνηθος, Suid. *s.v.* λυκόποδες. (3) περὶ τὴν Πάρνηθον, Schol. Ar. *Lys.* 666. (4) ὑπὸ τῆς Πάρνηθος, *Et. Mag.* p. 361. 32. (5) Herod. V. 62: Λειψύδριον τὸ ὑπὲρ Παιονίης τειχίσαντες. Aristotle is following Herodotus; perhaps in the original text of Herodotus stood the words ὑπὲρ Παιονίας ὑπὸ Πάρνηθος, which in the version that has reached us have been abbreviated into the incorrect ὑπὲρ Πάρνηθος. Paeonia — Paeonidae, not far from modern Menidhi — lay in the Attic πεδίον, north of Athens (Milchhöfer, *Text* to Curtius and Kaupert's *Attika*, II. 42); according to the explanation suggested above, Leipsydrium lay "beyond" it, on the southern slopes of Parnes. Aristotle, the Scholiasts, and the lexicographers make Leipsydrium a sort of earlier Phyle, whither the patriots of the sixth century fled and where they congregated. We may best explain the several statements by supposing that the Alcmeonidae fortified their ancient family home. The Alcmeonidae and the Paeonidae were cognate γένη, and must originally have dwelt near each other; Paeonia was the seat of the Paeonidae. Isocrates (XVI. 25) asserts that whenever the Peisistratidae conquered the Alcmeonidae, they levelled their houses to the ground and dug up their graves. Perhaps the scolion on Leipsydrium (see above, p. 43, note 1) refers in part to some such acts. Later members of the family of the Alcmeonidae, to be sure, come from Agryle (Leobates, Plut. *Them.* 23) and Alopece (*C.I.A.* I. 122; Aristot. *Respub. Ath.* c. 22), and from other demes of the πεδίον, not, however, in the vicinity of Leipsydrium, but near Athens. These cases, however, belong to post-Cleisthenean times; the new demes by no means stood for the ancient homes of families of the demotae. The members of an ancient family might well be scattered over Attica.

One might hazard the conjecture that it was as promoters of trade between Euboea and Athens — the chief route of which passed their doors — or perhaps as exporters of corn from their fertile inland estates that the Alcmeonidae originally came into relation with the Shoremen, a relation that grew more intimate as new foreign connexions, formed when the family went into exile, extended the range of their commercial activity. Aristotle seems to suggest Delphi as the source of the wealth of the family (*Respub. Ath.* c. 19, ὅθεν εὐπόρησαν, κ.τ.λ.). But the passage, besides being corrupt, is a faulty condensation of Herod. VI. 62 *ad fin.* and 63 *ad init.*

an identity of business interests, an identity that had been the slow growth of years.[1]

The beginnings of trade and industry in Attica[2] are hardly to be placed much earlier than the last third of the seventh century B.C. The primitive system of barter had prevailed hitherto. By the middle of the following century there was a vigorous trade with the west, in which Athens received grain in exchange for her pottery and for her silver. Solon's prohibition[3] of the export of all agricultural products of Attica — this cannot include manufactured articles — except oil, the supply of which alone exceeded the demand for local consumption, shows that before his legislation there had been extensive trading and an exportation by enterprising merchants of articles needed for home use. The corn trade, to be sure, was largely in the hands of Megara, which, like Corinth and Aegina, much anticipated Athens in commercial enterprise; and when the war with Megara closed this source of supply, distress was prevalent. But Athens herself launched her ships upon the seas, and now sought gain in foreign lands.[4] Indeed, it was probably with a view to securing something of the corn trade of the Black Sea that the Athenians were led, not long after Draco, to send an expedition, their first to cross the seas, so as to secure a foothold on the Hellespont in the Troad. Involved in a quarrel with Mytilene, which laid claim to the Troad as her own colonial territory (Aeolic), the Athenians succeeded, however, in maintaining their ground after the decisive capture of Sigeum.[5] The establishment of the naucraries,[6] which clearly had to do with the promotion of a navy, probably for the protection of the merchant marine, is unintelligible except upon

---

[1] The significance of the connexion of the family with the Parali reappears as late as the time of Pericles, whose son Paralus received his name probably in recognition of this relation, a name originally suggested, doubtless, by that of the Attic hero Paralus (Eur. *Suppl.* 659), himself, however, perhaps the mythical impersonation of the Parali. Cf. Stein, on Herod. I. 59. 16.

[2] On the whole subject, see Busolt, *G. G.* I. pp. 501 ff.; H. Droysen, *Athen u. d. Westen*, pp. 39-40.   [3] Plut. *Sol.* 24.

[4] Sol. *Frag.* 13. 43-46, cited in part above, p. 9, note 3.

[5] Strabo XIII. 599. The date of the operations before Sigeum was not far from B.C. 610: see above, p. 9, and note 5. The Sigean Inscription belongs to a date only a little later: Roberts, *Greek Epigr.* pp. 78, 334-6; Kirchhoff, *Studien zur Griech. Alphab.*[4] p. 22 ff. For Phrynon, the general, see above, p. 50, note 1.   [6] On the naucraries, see above, p. 31, note 1.

this supposition. We have good evidence that Solon himself engaged in trade, and the sagacity of his economical and financial reforms reveals a man practically acquainted with the intricacies and needs of business intercourse. The evident friendliness of Solon for the Alcmeonidae might possibly be explained on the supposition of a unity of interests with them in matters of trade.

The social distress in Attica which prevailed for a number of years before Solon's appearance upon the scene was due to a variety of causes. The long war with Megara not only had exhausted the resources of the people, but had forced the Athenians to get such imported corn as was needed as best they could, probably only at a great cost. The change from primitive traffic by barter to that of buying and selling with coined money would weigh very heavily upon the peasant, and even upon the landed proprietor who had no capital but his lands; increase and uncertainty in prices would naturally ensue, and a financial crisis would be precipitated. A third cause of discontent was found in the unjust manner with which the ruling families, in whose hands lay the judicial functions, executed judgment, favoring their friends and oppressing the helpless. The only persons who did not suffer in this order of things were the capitalists, who, in fact, throve in it. In some cases the capitalists were landed proprietors, but many of them must have got their money by trade. A landowner with money had the peasant at his mercy, and the result was not only that the country was dotted with slabs which served as records of mortgages, but that the holdings of land by single individuals vastly and unduly increased. Nay, more : so high was the rate of interest which it was possible to exact from starving debtors, that many of the unfortunates found it impossible to pay the principal and were thus sold into slavery, themselves or their children, in satisfaction for their debts.

Solon's reforms changed these conditions, and secured equity for every one. For our purposes it is unnecessary to dwell upon these reforms. It is enough to say that the χρεῶν ἀποκοπή, or absolute remission of debts, commonly known as the Seisachthy, and in fact the whole revolution, must have been highly objectionable to the capitalists,[1] who,

---

[1] In the words ὅλως δὲ διετέλουν νοσοῦντες τὰ πρὸς ἑαυτούς, οἱ μὲν ἀρχὴν καὶ πρόφασιν ἔχοντες τὴν τῶν χρεῶν ἀποκοπήν (συμβεβήκει γὰρ αὐτοῖς γεγονέναι πένη-

however, when once a financial and business settlement had been reached, preferred to allow it to remain rather than to risk losses by further revolution.[1]

It is an interesting fact that of the post-Solonian parties, — the Parali, Pediaei, Diacrii,[2] — the Parali is the party of law-abiding citizens, which stands intermediate between the two extremes of oligarchic and democratic agitators, and seeks the perpetuation of the *status quo.*[3] That the Parali were rich is apparent from the language of Plutarch,[4] and their wealth would show that they were something more than fisher-folk. Everything supports the hypothesis that they were traders as well ;[5] and the wealth, foreign alliances and connexions of the Alcmeonidae, the champions and representatives of this party, can best be explained on the supposition that they, too, were engaged in trade in a large and liberal manner.

It would probably require no little amount of time for a number of persons of identical business interests to transform their mercantile union into a political combination ; accordingly the party of the Parali must have been long in forming, and the wealth of the Alcmeonidae must have been well assured before Megacles assumed the leadership of the Parali.

The chronology of the early history of the house will gain further definiteness if we note a few matters in connexion with the life and

---

σιν), οἱ δὲ τῇ πολιτείᾳ δυσχεραίνοντες διὰ τὸ μεγάλην γεγονέναι μεταβολήν, ἔνιοι δὲ διὰ τὴν πρὸς ἀλλήλους φιλονικίαν (Aristot. *Respub. Ath.* c. 13), we probably have the capitalists, the ancient conservatives, and the rising anti-Alcmeonidean factions, reviving old family feuds.

[1] This may explain the readiness of the Parali (Megacles) to compromise.

[2] On the various forms of these names, see Landwehr, *Philol.* Suppl.-Bd. V. (1884), pp. 154 ff.

[3] Plut. *Sol.* 13 (οἱ Πάραλοι μέσον τινὰ καὶ μεμιγμένον αἱρούμενοι πολιτείας τρόπον, κ.τ.λ.; cf. 29) is of course only a paraphrase of Aristot. *Respub. Ath.* c. 13 (μία μὲν τῶν Παραλίων, ὧν προειστήκει Μεγακλῆς ὁ ᾽Αλκμέωνος, οἵπερ ἐδόκουν μάλιστα διώκειν τὴν μέσην πολιτείαν), itself drawn freely from Herod. I. 59.

[4] Plut. *Sol.* 29, of the party of Peisistratus, ἐν οἷς ἦν ὁ θητικὸς ὄχλυς καὶ μάλιστα τοῖς πλουσίοις ἀχθομένοις. Cf. also Polyaenus, I. 21. 3: Μεγακλῆς ὑπὲρ τῶν πλουσίων τεταγμένος, κ.τ.λ.

[5] In Aristot. *Respub. Ath.* c. 13 (εἶχον δ᾽ ἕκαστοι τὰς ἐπωνυμίας ἀπὸ τῶν τόπων ἐν οἷς ἐγεώργουν), ἐγεώργουν is not to be pressed in its literal sense; still, the lands of the traders would doubtless be mainly near the shore.

fortunes of this Megacles : viz. the probable date of his marriage with Agariste, daughter of the Sicyonian Cleisthenes, and of two or three of the episodes of his struggle with Peisistratus.

The house of the Orthagoridae ruled, or, as Plutarch would put it, chastised,[1] the Sicyonians for one hundred years,[2] evidently a round number intended to include three generations. Myron, the son of the founder, won an Olympic victory in the four-horse chariot-race in Ol. 33 (B.C. 648),[3] and his more illustrious grandson Cleisthenes won a Pythian victory in Ol. 49. 3 (B.C. 582).[4] The same Cleisthenes was by tradition one of the important participants in the First Sacred War.[5] As the length of his reign was about thirty years,[6] we may suppose him to have ruled from about 595 B.C. to 565 B.C. At some date within this period yet to be established, he gave his daughter Agariste in marriage to the young and wealthy Megacles, son of the Alcmeon whose acquaintance he had doubtless made in the operations before Crisa. The tale of this wedding as given by Herodotus has many fictitious elements in it, but the marriage itself is an undoubted historical fact.[7] One of the rejected suitors, the Philaïd Hippocleides, was archon in 566 B.C. (Ol. 53. 3)[8]; the wedding can hardly have taken place much less than ten years before this date. If Megacles's daughter, who became the wife of Peisistratus[9] about 550 B.C., was

---

[1] Plut. *De Sera Num. Vind.* 7 (*Mor.* 553 B). Cf. Herod. V. 67, ᾿Αδρηστον μὲν εἶναι Σικυωνίων βασιλέα, ἐκεῖνον δὲ λευστῆρα (Pythia, of Cleisthenes).

[2] [Aristot.] *Pol.* VIII. (V.) 12. (9), 21, p. 1315[b] 14. (pp. 587 ff. Susemihl). Cf. Busolt, *G. G.* I. p. 466, note 2.

[3] Paus. VI. 19. 2.

[4] Paus. X. 7. 6.

[5] Paus. II. 9. 6; X. 37. 6.

[6] Nicol. Damasc. 59 makes it thirty-one years.

[7] Herod. VI. 126–131. Cf. Zühlke, *De Agaristes Nuptiis* (Königsb. 1880); Busolt, *G. G.* I. pp. 466, 554; Töpffer, *Att. Gen.* p. 279, and Petersen, *Hist. Gent. Attic.* pp. 21, 83.

[8] Athen. XIV. 628 C, D. Hesych. and Suid. *s.v.* οὐ φροντίς. Archon, Ol. 53. 3: cf. Euseb. II. 94 (Syncell. p. 454. 8) with Marcell. *Thuc.* 3 (*i.e.* Pherecydes and Hellanicus, on the authority of Didymus), ῾Ιπποκλείδης ἐφ' οὗ ἄρχοντος Παναθήναια ἐτέθη. The family of Hippocleides was already connected with another ruling house, the Bacchiadae of Corinth. Stemmata are given by Petersen, *l.c.* p. 16, and Töpffer, *l.c.* p. 320.

[9] Cf. Herod. I. 60 and Aristot. *Respub. Ath.* c. 14; the latter, while following Herodotus closely, at times verbatim, gives fuller information upon the chro-

a child of this union, which seems highly probable, we gain another *terminus ante quem* for the date of the wedding ; viz. about B.C. 565. Herodotus also informs us that the wedding contests and the wedding took place in a year in which the Olympic games had been celebrated, where Cleisthenes had won a victory with the four-horse chariot. The dates that best satisfy all the conditions are B.C. 568, 572 or 576.[1]

The struggles of Megacles with Peisistratus and their mutual compromises furnish one or two additional chronological data of significance. Peisistratus established himself as tyrant for the first time, after a picturesque conflict with Megacles in the popular assembly,[2] in the

---

nology. Although there is some uncertainty as to the dates of Peisistratus and the Peisistratidae (cf. Busolt, *G. G.* I. 551, 552, and notes; Meiners, *Diss. Hal.* II, pp. 263 ff.; and Kenyon, note on Aristot. *l.c.*, who discuss the subject fully), the following conclusions may safely be drawn. Peisistratus established himself as tyrant in the archonship of Comeas, B.C. 561 or 560 (Comeas, archon : Phanias, *ap.* Plut. *Sol.* 32, makes this date B.C. 560–59; Mar. Par. Ep. 40, either B.C. 561–60 or 560–59, but Euseb. II. 94, Arm. Vers., 561–60). He was twice afterward deposed. Herodotus says that he was first ejected, μετὰ δὲ οὐ πολλὸν χρόνον ... τυραννίδα ... οὔπω κάρτα ἐρριζωμένην. Aristotle makes this period five years (ἔκτῳ ἔτει μετὰ τὴν πρώτην κατάστασιν, ἐφ' Ἡγησίου ἄρχοντος), and then says ἔτει δὲ δωδεκάτῳ μετὰ ταῦτα a reconciliation was effected with Megacles, whose daughter Peisistratus takes in marriage. If we take ταῦτα as referring to B.C. 556 or 555, the subsequent dates of Peisistratus are thrown into hopeless confusion. If, however, we take ταῦτα (wrongly written for ταύτην?) as referring to the πρώτην κατάστασιν above (but see p. 68, note 3), everything becomes consistent, and we are not forced to infer, with Kenyon, that Aristotle has made a blunder. On this supposition, the compromise with Megacles, and the marriage of his daughter, would have taken place about B.C. 550–49. Very soon, however, Peisistratus breaks with Megacles, and from this time dates the period of irreconcilable hostility between the Alcmeonidae and the house of Peisistratus, by Isocrates described roundly as forty years in length (τετταράκοντα δ' ἔτη τῆς στάσεως γενομένης, Isocr. XVI. 25), *i.e.* from 550 B.C. to 510 B.C. (expulsion of Hippias).

[1] I am unable to see the bearing of Busolt's remark (*G. G.* I. p. 466), which is true enough, that Cleisthenes the Athenian was born after 575 B.C., nor why this should show that the wedding could not have taken place as early as 576 B.C. I know of no evidence that shows that Cleisthenes was the first-born child, born soon after the marriage. Undoubtedly he was born some considerable time after 575 B.C.: he would not seem to have been an old man when he carried through his reforms (about 508–7 B.C.).

[2] This episode is not given by Herodotus nor by Aristotle, but by Polyaenus (I. 21. 3), very briefly, from an independent source.

archonship of Comeas (B.C. 561 or 560).[1] It was, then, before this date that the parties of the Parali, Diacrii, and Pediaei were in vigorous rivalry : these agitations succeeded by several years the two-year and two-month archonship of Damasias, which, according to Aristotle (*Respub. Ath.* c. 13), began at least ten years after the archonship of Solon ; Damasias having been expelled from office, a compromise was adopted by which a board of ten archons was chosen, five from the εὐπατρίδαι, three from the ἄποικοι (ἄγροικοι), and two from the δημιουργοί. Less than a score of years before B.C. 561, then, the strife of classes had merged into that of local factions. Peisistratus does not, however, long remain in secure possession of his power ; by a combination, according to Herodotus (I. 60), of the parties of Megacles and Lycurgus, he is driven out. Subsequently, however, — we are not in a position to establish the dates with accuracy, but probably about 550 B.C., — he compromises with Megacles, and receives his daughter in marriage as a token of cordial union. As Cylon had been son-in-law of a Megarian despot, so Peisistratus becomes the husband of the granddaughter of a Sicyonian ruler, though in all probability Cleisthenes was not living at this time. Aristotle (*Respub. Ath.* c. 17) points out that Peisistratus had secured foreign allies by his marriage with the Argive Timonassa ; by this alliance he may have hoped to win not alone the support of the powerful Megacles, but also the favor of the foreign Sicyonians.

Of the subsequent falling-out of Megacles and Peisistratus, and of the later uncompromising struggles between the family of Megacles and that of Peisistratus, of the services of the Alcmeonidae to art and religion in rebuilding the Delphian temple, and to political progress in the achievements of Cleisthenes, this is not the place to speak.

It remains to gather up the chronological data obtained in this examination of the evidence, and to draw the necessary inferences : —

Megacles II., married in 568 B.C., or before, at the head of a powerful political party as early as 565 B.C., was born not later than 595 B.C., and probably as early as 605 B.C. His father, Alcmeon, general in the Sacred War, was well on in years in 595 B.C., hardly less than forty or forty-five years of age. This would carry back the

---

[1] Cf. p. 58, note 9, above.

date, at which Alcmeon's father (Megacles I.) was in the prime of his powers and eligible for election to the archonship, to some point of time before Draco, much nearer to 640 B.C. than to 610 B.C.[1]

## VII.

### THEAGENES OF MEGARA.

THE age of Cylon, that of Alcmeon, and that of Megacles have thus furnished us some data for determining the time of Cylon's attempted usurpation. If we had it in our power, in a way equally independent, to establish the date of Theagenes, tyrant of Megara and father-in-law of Cylon, this fact would furnish additional considerations of much weight. Unfortunately the evidence on this point is both meagre and inadequate. Hitherto Theagenes has gained his date from Cylon, not Cylon from Theagenes, and there seems to be no direct evidence, except that which connects these two men, as to the date of the Megarian tyrant. Is there, however, nothing in the historical conditions, economic and political, of Megara that makes it most probable that Theagenes was in power as early as 640 B.C.?

In the industrial and commercial development of the states on and near the Saronic gulf, in the course of the seventh century B.C., a far greater activity prevailed at Epidaurus, Aegina, Corinth, Sicyon, and Megara than at Athens. Athens — and this is the political name of the people inhabiting the geographical district known as Attica[2] — was, as we have noted, actively engaged during this time in bringing into relation with herself the newly acquired state and district of Eleusis; she was rent by the opposing factions of great

---

[1] An argument, like the above, when it stands alone, has no convincing force; it suggests merely one of several possibilities, and it is only when all other seeming possibilities which are contradictory or inconsistent have been eliminated that one's possibility becomes a certainty. When, however, an argument of this sort reaches conclusions sustained by other and wholly independent courses of reasoning, the possibility that it urges becomes a probability, and the argument thus has value and weight.

[2] Hom. γ 278 ἄκρον 'Αθηνέων (of Sunium); Thuc. II. 93, and *passim*. "Seit Kleisthenes ist ἡ πόλις ἡ 'Αθηναίων ein ideeller begriff, gleich ὁ δῆμος ὁ 'Αθηναίων, und der bedeutungswechsel zwischen stadt und staat," Wilamowitz, *Phil. Unters.* I. p. 111.

families ; the people were slowly increasing in numbers, and domestic industries — the manufacture of pottery and the culture of the olive for its oil—were beginning to flourish. Thus engaged, and endowed with a land in which agriculture was on the whole a remunerative occupation, the Athenians, as a people, did not have occasion to concern themselves in the far-reaching commercial movements whereby, throughout this century and also through the last fifty years of the preceding century, the Greek name and civilization were spread over the shores of the Mediterranean and the Black Sea. In this activity Athens was far behind her sister states, and it was not until about the time of Solon that many of her citizens became interested in commercial enterprises.

With Corinth and Sicyon, and with Megara in particular, the case had been different. The latter state, as early as the first half of the seventh century, had sent powerful colonies to the Thracian Bosporus and had there founded the great cities of Chalcedon and Byzantium ; still earlier she had sent colonies to Sicily.[1] Now, such movements imply, at least in this period of Greek colonization, great inward agitation ; commercial activity is often the occasion as well as the result of domestic upheavals. The acquisition of wealth by industry and by trade — and the two necessarily go hand in hand — introduces into the social organism a new aristocracy, which ranges itself in opposition to the ancient aristocracy of birth, the wealth of which mainly lies in lands. The lines that separate classes thus grow fainter ; the masses of the common people, finding a source of abundant livelihood in the social occupations of industry and trade, as against the lonelier occupation of agriculture, become conscious of their common interests and common relations, and from union in occupation easily acquire and gradually develop a sense of union in political concerns.

It thus happened, as an historical fact, that in this period of activity in colonization, the states that were most prominent were precisely the states that underwent the most radical political revolutions. The ancient conservative aristocracy, that in the eighth century B.C. had gradually and apparently without revolution taken the place of the rule of kings, now underwent rapid and signal

---

[1] Chalcedon in 675 B.C., and Byzantium in 659 B.C. See Busolt, *G. G.* I. pp. 326, 327, for the authorities.

transformation; the new aristocracy of wealth — and wealth, according to Aristotle, is the essential feature of oligarchy [1] — supplanted the older aristocracy of family. The people meantime became restive, and were ripe for a change. The political agitations that ensue sprung in part from the consciousness in the people of increased power, with a growing discontent at the existing state of affairs and a resentment at the oppression to which in the unequal contests of the times they were subject, and in part from the factional quarrels of the ruling oligarchic aristocrats, the families of which were no longer held by ancient ties. These agitations commonly issue in one of two political conditions. In the conflict between people and aristocrats, the aristocrats yield in part, and by way of compromise αἰσυμνῆται [2] are chosen as arbiters, whose main duty it is to make record of the ancient law which in the troublous times was wrested by its administrators — the aristocratic rulers and judges — to the hurt of the people. Another and perhaps more frequent result is that some member of the leading families in power takes up the cause of the people, and sustained by the people rebels against the sway of his fellow-oligarchs, and thereby establishes himself as sole ruler or tyrant. The period of the rule of the oligarchs, before it received modification by the activity of the aesymnetae or was supplanted by that of tyrants, was usually a brief period — at least in commercial states. The history of Corinth and of Sicyon in particular illustrate these propositions, and from the *Politics* of Aristotle one may gather additional examples.

What bearing have these considerations upon the date of Theagenes? As the period of Corinth's greatest colonial activity was coincident with that of the rule of the Cypselidae; as at Sicyon the Orthagoridae held sway throughout all this period of commercial and industrial activity, it is natural to suppose that similar changes and states were found under precisely similar conditions at Megara, — in other words, we must infer that the tyranny of Theagenes, and its successful establishment, are to be placed nearer 650 B.C. than 621 B.C.

---

[1] Aristot. *Pol.* VI. (IV.) 4, 7, p. 1290$^b$ 1; *ib.* VI. (IV.) 8, 4, p. 1294$^a$ 11; *Rhet.* I. 8, 5, p. 1366$^a$ 5.

[2] Aristot. *Pol.* III. 14. (9), 5, p. 1285$^a$ 31; *ib.* VI. (IV.) 10, 2, p. 1295$^a$ 14. Busolt, *G. G.* I. pp. 438, 439.

At Sicyon certainly some time before 650 B.C. the Orthagoridae are well established; for it was in 648 B.C. that Myron, son of the ruling tyrant, won an Olympic victory,[1] — a victory which may have spurred the ambition of the youthful Cylon. At Corinth before 650 B.C.[2] Cypselus was in the full possession of power; and a date certainly not more than ten years later must be ascribed to Procles,[3] the cruel despot of Epidaurus. As early as 640 B.C., then, Theagenes would have had at any rate precedents enough for making himself master of Megara.

Certain features in the subsequent history of Megara are somewhat more intelligible if we ascribe to Theagenes an early date rather than a late one. At a date considerably preceding the archonship of Solon, Megara had begun her efforts to subjugate Athens. The first step, an insidious one, may have been Cylon's attempt, at a time when Athens and Megara would seem to have been on good terms; this was followed, as a second step, by a long war for the possession of Salamis; Megara in this war was successful, gained the island and colonized it, — only at a considerably later period being obliged to give it up. Commercial rivalry is not, at this time, a sufficient ground to explain this contest over Salamis, at least in its earlier stages,

---

[1] After his victory he erected at Olympia the treasury of the Sicyonians (Paus. VI. 19. 1, 2), in which were two θάλαμοι. The recent excavations at Olympia have discovered the θησαυρὸς Σικυονίων, not, however, in its original form; the inscriptions (Roehl, *I.G.A.* pp. 171, 172, No. 27 *b, c*) are not earlier than the end of the sixth century B.C. Cf. Bötticher, *Olympia*, pp. 215 ff.; Busolt, *G. G.* I. p. 467, 468, note 3.

[2] According to Ephorus and Apollodorus (inferred from Diod. Sic. VII. *Frag.* 9), Cypselus began his reign 657 B.C. Busolt, *G. G.* I. pp. 333, 447.

[3] Procles married, for political reasons, the daughter of Aristocrates of Orchomenus, who was slain about 640 B.C., of course before her father's death; their daughter Lyside became the wife of Periander of Corinth, and was thereafter named Melissa. Periander came into power about B.C. 625: he was tyrant for forty years. As the sons and daughters of his union with Melissa were grown up, and also, on the other hand, as Melissa died in pregnancy at the time when Periander fell out with his aged father-in-law and subjugated Epidaurus to Corinth, we cannot place the conquest of Epidaurus much before or much after B.C. 600 (Periander was nearly seventy in 600 B.C., since he died in 585, eighty years of age: Diog. Laert. I. 7. 95, 98, but see Diels, *Rhein. Mus.* 31 [1876], pp. 19, 20). Procles, then, would seem to have made himself tyrant of Epidaurus before 640 B.C. Cf. Duncker, *Gesch. d. Alterthums*, VI.[5] pp. 51, 52.

Athens as yet not having distinctly become a commercial state. The high-handed proceedings of the Megarians are such, one may venture to believe, as would be undertaken by a state ruled by an ambitious man, and not by a people engaged in trade and rapidly growing rich, enjoying a peaceful aristocratic regime. In the later stages of this long struggle with Megara, initiated on personal grounds, the sense of commercial rivalry added a spur to the intensity with which the contest was carried on. As we have already remarked, the attempt of Athens to gain a foothold in the Hellespont was in part intended as a menace to Megara. It was also doubtless a feeling of rivalry with Megara as a formidable competitor that brought Athens and Corinth into close commercial union at this early date.[1] If the attempt of Cylon had proved successful, Athens would have become a subject state of Dorian Megara, and the subsequent history of Hellenic civilization would have been vastly different from what it actually became. Athens, however, was not now ripe for a tyrant; the people had not yet gained that consciousness of their own power, combined with a feeling of helplessness before their masters, that would lead them to range themselves against their ancient rulers on the side of a young, half-foreign adventurer.

Finally, the condition of things at Megara in the middle of the sixth century B.C., *i.e.* at the time of Theognis, who reflects it in his elegiacs, would presuppose a long period of social disintegration and disorder. Theagenes seems to have raised himself into power by championing the interests of the poor country folk as against certain wealthy landed proprietors. Aristotle[2] informs us that on behalf of the humbler folk he slew the herds of the rich that were grazing in the river-meadows, which were naturally the property of the poor but had been appropriated by the rich. There is, however, no evidence that Theagenes's power rested upon a general uprising of all the lower classes against the ruling aristocracy. His rule was beneficent, and to him were ascribed, doubtless correctly, certain great public works that

---

[1] The adoption, at this early period, by the Athenians, of the Euboeic standard, bound Athens more closely to Corinth-Chalcis, and aided in bringing about mercantile emancipation from Aegina and Megara. Cf. Busolt, *G. G.* I. pp. 460, 461, and *Griech. Staatsalt.* (I. Müller, *Handb.* IV.) p. 114.

[2] Aristot. *Pol.* VIII. (V.) 4 (5), 5, p. 1305ᵃ 24; cf. also *Rhet.* I. 2. 7, 1357ᵇ 33.

were the pride of Megara.[1] Of the length of his reign we have no information; it was followed by a mild regime in which power was exercised by the aristocrats,[2] and then came little by little the dreadful social disorganization and demoralization that saddens the verses of Megara's patriot-poet. To Theognis[3] the most painful feature of the new order of things is that it is the base-born rich that have supreme influence and power, and that society is turned completely upside down. It may safely be asserted that so many changes in the political system, and so complete a revolution in the very social order, could hardly have been wrought within the compass of a few decades.

## VIII.

### THE DATE OF EPIMENIDES.

The only objections that can be offered to an early date for Cylon, not already incidentally considered, are based upon the alleged connexion of the Cretan Epimenides with the ceremonies that attended the purification of Athens from a pestilence visited upon the city, presumably because of the Cylonian sacrilege. According to certain late writers (among them probably Hermippus, apparently quoted by Plutarch in *Sol.* 12), the city was disturbed by superstitious fears and strange appearances; the priests declared that the sacrifices intimated some villanies and pollutions not yet expiated. Hereupon Epimenides was sent for; he not only purified the city by various lustrations, but by his new ordinances humanized the people and rendered service to religion and justice, thereby preparing the way for Solon.[4] Now the date of the visit of Epimenides to Athens is by some authorities — whom many classical historians follow — given as Ol. 46 (596-2 B.C.).[5] Hence, it has been inferred, the Cylonian attempt

---

[1] Paus. I. 40. 1 and 41. 2, of a fountain in Megara, with its extensive aqueduct.

[2] Plut. *Quaest. Graec.* 18 (*Mor.* 265 D).

[3] Theognis, 53–60, 289–93, etc. Theognis Ol. 59. 4: Euseb. II. 98.

[4] Further details about Epimenides's work are given in Diog. Laert. I. 10. 110–112. Plutarch ascribes to Epimenides well-known Solonian ordinances (*e.g.* the sumptuary regulations as to funerals, etc.). Cf. Niese (*Zur Gesch. Solons*, p. 13), who demonstrates the fabulous character of much that is ascribed to Epimenides.

[5] Diog. Laert. I. 10. 110 (Ol. 46); Euseb. (Jerome), II. 93 (Abrah. year 1422 = B.C. 595, Ol. 46. 2). See Busolt, *G. G.* I. p. 509, for the literature before

must have preceded this date by only a short time, and should be placed at the nearest convenient Olympic year.

Now, as will soon be shown, this whole story of the connexion of Epimenides with the affair of Cylon may be a fiction, and yet, even if the substantial truth of it be granted, the inference by no means follows that Cylon's attempted usurpation took place only a short time before the visit of Epimenides to Athens. Plutarch (*Sol.* 12) expressly asserts that the affair had for a long time been disturbing the state before remedial measures were resorted to, and his ἐκ πολλοῦ in its connexion is much more likely to connote forty years than four. Again, even those ancient writers who maintained that Epimenides visited Athens in Ol. 46 were not unanimous in asserting that the cause of this visit, according to Epimenides himself,[1] was the Κυλώ-νειον ἄγος.[2] Plutarch's language also is inconsistent with itself: all

---

1885. Little weight is to be attached to this date, Ol. 46; it is evidently not based on ἀναγραφαί, but is due to the conjectural combinations of the later chronographers. See p. 68, notes 2 and 3, below.

[1] One well-known apparent point of contact between the Κυλώνειον ἄγος and Epimenides is that referred to in Cicero *De Legg.* 2. 11. 28, and Clem. Alex. *Ad Gent.* II. 26. It appears that near the precinct of the σεμναὶ θεαί, *i.e.* between the western slope of the Acropolis and the Areopagus, but nearer the latter, was the Κυλώνειον, presumably the spot where the sacrilege was committed (Polemon *ap.* Schol. Soph. *O. C.* 489, Codd. Κυδώνιον). Probably here also were the two ancient stones, known as the stones of Violence and of Pitilessness, whereupon, before the court of the Areopagus, accused and accuser used respectively to stand (Paus. I. 28. 5, Ὕβρεως καὶ Ἀναιδείας λίθους). In the later tradition these stones appear to be turned into altars: so Theophrastus (Θεόφραστος ἐν τῷ περὶ νόμων Ὕβρεως καὶ Ἀναιδείας παρὰ τοῖς Ἀθηναίοις εἶναι βωμούς, Zenob. 4. 36). Ister, however, writing after Theophrastus, and possibly quoting him by name, makes Ἀναίδεια have a temple (Ἱερόν) at Athens (Suid. *s.v.* Θεὸς ἡ Ἀναίδεια). It is probable that Ister, if not Theophrastus whom Cicero may have known at first hand (*De Off.* 2. 18), is the authority for *De Legg.* 2. 11. 28: "nam illud vitiosum Athenis, quod Cylonis scelere expiato Epimenide Crete suadente fecerunt Contumeliae fanum et Impudentiae [better, Implacabilitatis]." The earlier form of statement (βωμούς) reappears in Clem. Alex. *l.c.* It is highly probable that the part ascribed to Epimenides in this matter is merely an attempt to bring into connexion the Κυλώνειον and the two stones, the story arising only when the ancient use of the stones had been long forgotten. These stones may originally have been merely venerable fetishes.

[2] Diog. Laert. I. 10. 110: οἱ δὲ τὴν αἰτίαν εἰπεῖν [*sc.* Ἐπιμενίδην] τοῦ λοιμοῦ τὸ Κυλώνειον ἄγος.

the commotion and disorder ceased with the departure of the Alcmeonidae, and yet afterward came Epimenides and allayed the
disorders.[1]

Both of the arguments given above presuppose that the date of
Epimenides's visit is correctly given in the tradition cited. Aristotle
gives yet another tradition, which is possibly also at the bottom of
some of Suidas's chronological data;[2] according to this the visit of
Epimenides must have taken place a dozen or a score of years
before Ol. 46.[3] Good reasons, however, have been offered of late

---

[1] Plut. *Sol.* 13. Cf. Niese, *Zur Gesch. Solons*, p. 13, note 3. Thuc. (I. 126)
appears to believe that the banishment of the Alcmeonidae was deemed a sufficient atonement for the ἄγος.

[2] Suidas, *s.v.* 'Επιμενίδης, gives a farrago of information, in which, however, lurk
some interesting points. We are told that Epimenides was born Ol. 30 (*i.e.*, 660–
56 B.C.) and that he purified Athens of the Cylonian taint Ol. 44 ($\mu\delta' = 604$–00).
Now the ancient chronographers, in dealing with periods and persons not attested
by recorded documents (ἀναγραφαί, etc.) followed two principles, that of ἀκμή and
that of synchronism (Diels, *Rhein. Mus.* 31 [1876], pp. 12–15). The ἀκμή fell forty
years after birth: the memorable deed of the persons whose dates were investi-
gated marked the ἀκμή. Thus, in many such cases the birth-year given is exactly
forty years before the characteristic, and in some cases datable, deed. With
Epimenides we must take the reverse step: his birth is given B.C. 660–56; hence
his great deed — doubtless the purification of Athens — fell about B.C. 620–16.
But as the synchronistic principle was also at work with the chronographers, this
date — according to our view, a correct one, if Epimenides had any share whatever in the Cylonian business — is tampered with. Solon and Epimenides must be
brought together; in reconciling the two traditions, Suidas's source, as it were,
strikes the balance between 620 and 594, and fixes upon 604 as the date of
Epimenides's visit.

[3] Aristotle (*Respub. Ath.* c. 1) distinctly connects Epimenides with the affair
of Cylon, but it would be doing violence to the obvious sense of his language to suppose that the visit of Epimenides was as late as Solon's archonship: between the
mention of Epimenides and that of Solon the narrative describes the Draconian
constitution, the ancient pre-Draconian state, and the political and economic
agitations that preceded Solon's appearance upon the scene. — We must not,
however, press μετὰ ταῦτα, and infer that Epimenides's visit preceded Draco (c. 1,
*ad init.*); these words — in accordance with a usage of which other examples
may be noted at cc. 14 (see above, p. 58, note 9), 19 *ad init.*, 22 (p. 58, line
2, Kenyon), 26 (p. 74, l. 2), 28 (p. 78, l. 7), 38 *ad init.* (?) — seem to refer, over
the intervening clause about Epimenides, to the important statement preceding,
in this passage, the Cylonian affair. Thus, while Cylon must have preceded
Draco, it does not necessarily hold true that Epimenides's purification did. At

for believing that the story of the visit of Epimenides to Athens at this time, if not the actual existence of the Cretan sage, is pure fiction.

The earlier sources (Herodotus and Thucydides) have nothing whatever to say of Epimenides, either directly or by implication. The first appearance of the name of the Cretan in Greek literature is in Plato's *Laws* (I. 642 D), where it is said that he visited Athens ten years before the beginning of the Persian wars to carry out certain sacrifices ordered by the Delphic god; he also prophesied that the Persian wars would not take place for ten years. According to the tradition in Diogenes Laertius (I. 10. 110), Epimenides visited Athens in part to bring an end to a pestilence. Now an inscription said to belong to about 500 B.C. has come to light which shows that a pestilence prevailed in Athens about this time.[1] Combining all these data, Löschcke[2] has drawn the inference that Epimenides was an historical personage who actually visited Athens and rendered her signal service a few years before the beginning of the Persian wars. This ingenious hypothesis has been widely adopted, and Busolt[3] has suggested how the story might have become applied to the events of the former century: the pestilence of 500 B.C. might have been explained by the enemies of Cleisthenes as due to the Κυλώνειον ἄγος. Diels,[4] however, on the strength of Aristotle's language, reverses

---

the same time, it is highly improbable that Epimenides visited Athens very long after Draco.

It appears, then, that one tradition, which Aristotle follows, connected Epimenides with the purification of Athens for the Cylonian sacrilege not very many years after the crime. Another tradition brought Epimenides into relation with Solon. Solon's chief activity was in Ol. 46; hence the later chronographers, to give expression to this synchronism, assign the visit of Epimenides to Ol. 46. Yet another, evidently late, form of the legend combines the two traditions, and makes both Solon and Epimenides active in the measures adopted for the deliverance of the state from the Cylonian crime, the former in the trial, the two in co-operation in the ritual purifications (Plut. *Sol.* 12).

[1] *C.I.A.* I. 475: [λοι]μῷ θανούσης εἰμὶ [σῆ]μα Μυρ⟨ρ⟩ίνης. This inscription seems, however, to belong to a much earlier date, being, perhaps, as old as the psephism (*C.I.A.* IV. 1 *a*) relating to the cleruchs on Salamis, the oldest Attic decree extant (perhaps 570–60 B.C.). Roberts, *Greek Epigr.* p. 84.

[2] Löschcke, *Die Enneakrunosepisode bei Pausanias*, pp. 24 ff.

[3] Busolt, *G. G.* I. p. 510.

[4] Diels, *Ueber Epimenides von Kreta* (*Sitzungsb. d. Berl. Akad.* 1891, pp. 387–403).

Löschcke's proposition: the historic, actual Epimenides visited Athens not very long before Solon, to purify the city of the results of the Cylonian sacrilege, and, as the religious reformer of Athens, became associated, in the later legends, with Solon, her great political reformer. Later on, however, when the renewal of the Alcmeonidean ἄγος in Cleisthenes's time had revived the memory of the ancient seer, the name of Epimenides was attached to several Orphic forgeries and spurious oracles produced under and after the Peisistratidae, and this connexion gave rise to the tradition of his activity at Athens ten years before the Persian wars, which reappears in Plato: it also explains the story of his extraordinarily long life.

Whichever of these views [1] we may accept, — and that of Diels is extremely attractive, especially if we modify it to the extent of placing Epimenides's visit to Athens at about 615 B.C., — it is undeniably true that there are altogether too many mythical features about the stories of the Cretan sage — his preternaturally long life, his sleep of many years, his prophecies to the Athenians of the Persian wars and of the disasters connected with Munichia, to the Spartans of their defeat at Orchomenus, his alleged oracles,[2] etc., etc., — too many contradictory stories about his work and date,[3] to make it necessary for us to give much, if any, weight to considerations based upon the time of his supposed visit to Athens.[4]

---

[1] Löschcke's hypothesis has recently been examined by Töpffer (*Att. Geneal.*, 1889, pp. 141–5), who gives reasons for maintaining, with Niese, that the figure of the Cretan Epimenides belongs wholly to the domain of myth.

[2] Diog. Laert. I. 10. 109–115; Plut. *Sol.* 12; Paus. II. 21. 3. For some of these stories Theopompus may have been the source. Is not the reference to Munichia (ἰδόντα γοῦν τὴν Μουνιχίαν παρ' Ἀθηναίοις ἀγνοεῖν φάναι αὐτοὺς ὅσων κακῶν αἴτιον ἔσται τοῦτο τὸ χωρίον αὐτοῖς, Diog. Laert. *l.c.* 114) now made more intelligible by the statement, in Aristot. *Respub. Ath.* c. 19, of the circumstance not elsewhere mentioned, that Hippias endeavored to fortify Munichia, and that while thus engaged he was thwarted by the Spartan Cleomenes, this being the first, but by no means the last, instance of Spartan interference with Athens?

[3] As Diels suggests, speaking of Aristotle's mention of Epimenides, "die chronologisch unbestimmte Art, wie sein [Epimenides] Auftreten an die Process gegen die Alkmeoniden angeknüpft wird, zeigt dass ihm kein genaueres Datum zuverlässig überliefert war " (*l.c.* p. 392).

[4] Two additional objections that might be urged are only apparent. (1) Boeckh's assertion (*Pind.* II. 2, p. 304) that the Cylonian Megacles was archon in B.C. 599, because winner at Olympia Ol. 47 is based upon an assumption

# IX.

## RESULTS.

IF the conclusion be correct to which all these considerations bring us, — viz. that Cylon sought to make himself tyrant of Athens not later than 624 B.C. and perhaps as early as 636 B.C., — and if the various positions that we have taken in the course of our enquiry be well taken, it becomes important and interesting, finally, to note the place that the episode of Cylon will thus hold in the social and political changes of Athens in the last half of the seventh century B.C. and in the first half of the sixth century B.C. The case must have been somewhat as follows :

In the family rivalries for pre-eminence in the conduct of the Athenian state that prevailed about 640 B.C. and onward, the ancient and aristocratic family of Cylon forms a powerful alliance with a foreign prince who had designs on Athens.[1] Cylon, youthful and ambitious, misinterpreting the signs of the times, failing to see that the social conditions of his native city were not ripe for his enterprise, as those of Megara had been for that of his father-in-law, with the help of foreign troops[2] and of hairbrained comrades seizes the acropolis in his attempt to make himself ruler of Athens. The people, still in the main true to the ancient regime,[3] though pregnant with the spirit of revolution,

---

which he himself gives up (see above, p. 51, note 1). (2) The presence in current chronological hand-books of the name of Megacles as archon opposite the years B.C. 612, 599, or elsewhere. There is no evidence for the date of Megacles as archon except that based upon his connexion with the affair of Cylon, given above; in other words, it is the date that we adopt for Cylon that fixes the date for Megacles, not the reverse.

[1] Schömann suggests that the naucraries, then newly established, aroused the suspicions of Megara (*Jahrb. f. Philol.* 111 [1875], p. 455).

[2] As Sparta aided Hippias, more than a hundred years later (Herod. V. 91), and the Thirty, more than two hundred years later (Xen. *Hellen.* II. 3; Aristot. *Respub. Ath.* c. 34, *ad fin.*).

[3] May not the several stages of differentiation in the social body at Athens be briefly summed up as follows? (1) The ancient regime, the whole people living in contentment with members of the old leading γένη as their rulers. (2) A gradual differentiation of the residents of the city from those of the country : ἀστοί (including the rulers, for whom, though in some few cases actually resident in the country, the city was the political centre) as against ἄποικοι. (3) Sharp demarcation

hasten to subdue the adventurous youth; they are aided, perhaps led, by the family of the Alcmeonidae, now happily represented on the board of chief magistrates, who find a peculiar satisfaction in humiliating the formidable family of Cylon. The insurrection is wholly suppressed, the people having taken a prominent part in the movement. This activity on the part of the people, which like an electric shock has united them in a deepened consciousness of common danger and of common interests, leads them as a next step, —also in view of the stress of certain economic conditions, which only by Solon's day became absolutely unendurable, — to demand concessions from the ruling classes, at least to the extent that the laws should be recorded; for hitherto the laws have been written only in part and subject in their interpretation to the whims of rulers which are selected by members of the old families from their own numbers and unite in themselves executive and judicial functions. The concession is granted. In B.C. 624–0 Draco conducts the commission for the codification of the laws. As he appears to have been a duly elected magistrate, though probably not the chief archon, at least at the beginning, it was unnecessary to appoint him a special officer (aesymnete), as was commonly done elsewhere in similar cases. Draco yields to the popular demand, and proposes a new constitution, which, with all its novel and democratic features, has still somewhat of an aristocratic, if not plutocratic, stamp. For a time things go smoothly at home, though the little state has become

---

between ruling γένη (εὐπατρίδαι?), artisan class — mainly in the city, — and peasant folk (εὐπατρίδαι, δημιουργοί, ἄποικοι [ἄγροικοι or γεωμόροι]). From the permanent nature of such a differentiation when once commercial and other conditions had brought it about, whereby it long remained a social if not a political division, later generations would ascribe to it great antiquity. Thus Plut. *Thes.* 25, apparently quoting Aristotle, makes Theseus the founder of these class distinctions. (4) Local factions (Parali, Pediaei, Diacrii), in which the old lines of social demarcation were largely, though by no means wholly, obliterated, and were crossed by new ones arising in part from local, in part from family, and in part from class, interests. (5) Finally, as society becomes more and more united, as its various members come into closer contact geographically, economically, politically, it gradually falls asunder into its two grand divisions of the Few and the Many, the Well-to-do and the Populace. This principle of division is, of course, at work in the earliest stages, and lies at the bottom of them all, but it now becomes practically the only principle at work.

embroiled in a war with Megara for the possession of Salamis, which began doubtless immediately after Cylon's attempt and was but one step in the efforts of Theagenes to gain control of Athens; this war continues long, and its bitterness is intensified by the growing feeling of commercial rivalry between the two states. Athens, finally, unsuccessful nearer home, attempts by her new fleet and with new commercial enterprise to check the foreign power of her nearest foe by establishing herself on the Hellespont; Salamis, however, she is at last obliged to forego, and recovers the island only much later.[1] In all these anti-Megarian movements it is not surprising that the Cylonian party should continue to be in the background, but in time something of a reaction sets in: the family and friends of the surviving but exiled members of Cylon's party, still powerful at home, bestir themselves. They rally to their side all the factions that are hostile to or jealous of the Alcmeonidae, who thus early have figured, though by no means wholly disinterestedly, as champions of the humbler classes. The Alcmeonidae and their supporters are not as yet strong enough to meet this reactionary movement; in the conflict that ensues, the Alcmeonidae are sacrificed, and after a formal trial voluntarily go into exile. In exile they form powerful connexions both at home and abroad with Athenian traders and with foreign princes, and perhaps at Delphi with the far-seeing priesthood; they engage in trade, laying

---

[1] Plutarch (*Sol.* 8–10, and 12) speaks of two losses of Salamis: one, when the island, with Nisaea the seaport of Megara, was surrendered to Megara, presumably long after the Cylonian affair, and afterward recovered by Solon (αὐτὸς κῆρυξ ἦλθον, κ.τ.λ.); the other, just after the Cylonian affair. Herodotus (I. 59) makes Peisistratus prominent in the reconquest of Nisaea, and Aristotle (*Respub. Ath.* c. 14) follows him. Aristotle, however, denies (*Respub. Ath.* c. 17) that Peisistratus could have been general (στρατηγεῖν) in the Megarian war, — probably because he was not old enough to hold that office; Aristotle does not here necessarily refer to a pre-Solonian struggle, as Ad. Bauer (*l.c.*, p. 57, note) asserts. It seems probable, therefore, in view of these statements and of other serious chronological difficulties, that only one war for the recovery of Salamis took place, and this after Solon's legislation; in this the youthful Peisistratus won distinction. (See also Niese, *Zur Gesch. Solons*, pp. 21–24.) The ancient psephism referred to above (p. 69, note 1), touching Athenian cleruchs on Salamis (not later than 570–60 B.C.), would presuppose a conquest of the island, if not immediately, only a short time, before its enactment, when certain abuses that had lately arisen called for immediate correction.

thus the foundations of their great wealth. The trial and banishment may have taken place as early as 615 B.C., and perhaps the Hellespontine operations of Athens are undertaken at the instance of the alert exiles, who see in them not only a measure of great advantage to Athenian commerce, but also a party-stroke that will serve them a good turn at home against the friends of Cylonian faction. Life at Athens is not stagnant. The people, not only the lowest class, but the traders and the fisher-folk, the peasants, and the artisans, now, perhaps, for the first time so differentiated, gain in importance and power. In the reforms of Solon, carried through mainly in the interest of the people, and particularly of the peasant class, we have an evidence that the people, though down-trodden and degraded through the operation of economic forces, have enough power to constrain the state to make ample provision for their needs. In the meantime, evidently before the archonship of Solon, the aristocratic factions that have supported the cause of the Cylonians fall into the background, while the counter party is restored to favor. The Alcmeonidae return from exile ; and in due time their tried leader, rich, powerful, the friend of princes, the Alcmeonid Alcmeon, son of the bloodstained Megacles, gains so much of consideration in the eyes of the people and of their advocate Solon, that he becomes their leader and representative in the holy war for the honor of Delphi. In the controversies that soon follow, it is another Alcmeonid, a second Megacles, who, as the head of the Men of the Shore, champions the cause not only of his associates in business enterprises, but also of the great law-abiding middle class in its struggles for supremacy with the party of the ancient aristocracy, headed by Lycurgus, and with the proletariat, whom Peisistratus, himself also a member of an ancient family, for his own purposes was willing to lead.

Thus viewed, the episode of Cylon ceases to be a detached incident in Attic history : it now reveals itself, in its true light, as one of the most interesting and significant steps in the social and political development of pre-Solonian Athens.

# GENERAL INDEX.

———◦⊙◦———

# INDEX OF CITATIONS.

www.ingramcontent.com/pod-product-compliance
Lightning Source LLC
Chambersburg PA
CBHW032359020726
47499CB00008B/2816